◐ Report

Just Work:
Humanising the Labour Market in a Changing World

Paul Bickley and Barbara Ridpath

Acknowledgements

We would like to offer thanks to individuals and organisations that have encouraged, supported or assisted on this project. In particular, we are grateful for the generous support of our funders, including CCLA.

A number of Theos colleagues have contributed to the project – either by reading and commenting on drafts, or with communications. Madeleine Pennington, Nick Spencer, Lizzie Harvey, Hannah Rich, Abbie Allison, Emily Downe and Anna Wheeler all deserve a mention. However, we are particularly grateful to Peter Whitehead for his research input.

Malcolm Brown, Maria Exall, Tim Thorlby and Simon Cross were kind enough to read and comment on a draft of the report.

We would like to thank those that contributed to three roundtables for this project:

Stefan Stern (journalist and author of *How To Be A Better Leader*)

Soulla Kyriacou (Blueprint for Better Business)

Fiona Stewart Darling (Canary Wharf Chaplaincy)

Simon Cross (Office of the Bishop of Oxford)

Maria Exall (Honorary Fellow Centre for Catholic Social Thought and Practice at Durham University and Communication Workers Union)

Rebecca McDonald (Joseph Rowntree Foundation)

Malcolm Brown (Mission and Public Affairs, Church of England)

Sarah Bennett (EMEA Risk Business Unit Manager at Citigroup and Co-Chair Citi Women London)

Nick Dalton (author of *Change the Workplace, Change the World: The HR Revolution*)

Joanna Moriarty (Green Park Executive Search)

Tim Thorlby (Clean for Good)

Ruth Yeoman (Fellow of Kellogg College, University of Oxford and Associate Professor of Business Ethics, Northumbria University)

Their thoughtful discussions contributed significantly to the project. We are also grateful to David Goodhart, Dan Howard, and Thomas Yap for speaking at these roundtables.

Contents

Contents

This Report in 30 Seconds	6
Three Key Proposals	8
Executive Summary and Recommendations	11
Introduction	17
1 What is Work?	35
2 Humanising Work	50
3 Limiting Work	73
Conclusion	92

This Report in 30 Seconds

Work is not just necessary. It is a human good: it connects us to prosperity, to community, and gives meaning.

Currently, the world of work is facing three great disruptions: the technological (AI, machine learning, and automation); the ecological (climate change, loss of biodiversity); and anthropological (human vulnerability – seen through the pandemic, migration, and declining birth rates). Any of these would see many jobs eliminated, replaced, or changed. Together they create an unpredictable environment in which work could be dehumanised – or, we could seize these disruptions as an opportunity to humanise work and working conditions.

As the relationship between work, time, and place changes, there is a need to rediscover patterns of rest for human beings and for ecosystems.

6
Three Key Proposals

1. Paid employment is the main – but not the only – form of work. Paid employment is the way in which most people share in collective wealth, but unpaid work is also crucial to a flourishing society. We should recognise caring responsibilities and volunteer work as important forms of work. Our collective aim should be a "full work" rather than "full employment" economy, recognising the need both to distribute paid employment better and to duly acknowledge, create space for, and properly support unpaid but essential forms of work.

2. All stakeholders need to recognise the human priority in work. Investors, and first and foremost church investors, have achieved tangible changes through activism in areas such as climate change and governance. They should add clear requirements on the fair handling of wages, benefits, agency work, outsourcing, and employee surveillance to the social criteria they look at within environmental, social, and governance investing. While governments have a role in setting the conditions in which good jobs with fair conditions become the norm (see below), the nature of global markets means that national governments are not always the most powerful actors.

3. Dissolving boundaries between employment and leisure – exacerbated during the pandemic – have negatively affected many workers. The biblical idea of a Sabbath is an ancient answer to a very modern anxiety. If we could recover it, or find new shared practices of rest, we would help tackle overwork of people and exploitation of our natural environment. We recommend (1) that the UK should hold more public holidays; (2) we should look for ways to eliminate at least some of the vast quantity

of unpaid overtime in the economy (including by encouraging employers to pay overtime, so that the costs of work over and above legal hours are made explicit; this would have the added benefit of helping to maintain employment, as employers would have to increase hiring numbers to avoid paying 1.5x–2x overtime rates); and (3) support for the Living Hours campaign of the Living Wage Foundation.

Executive Summary

Work in a changing world

— This report seeks to consider contemporary issues around the status and future of work set within the framework of Christian thinking and practice. Debates around the future of work are framed economically, but this report affirms the wider moral, emotional, and even spiritual dimensions of these issues. It draws on Christian reflection on the nature of work as a basis through which to engage some of today's challenges facing the world of work.

— Work is facing three waves of disruption – the technological (AI, machine learning, automation and worker surveillance), the ecological (climate change, loss of biodiversity), and anthropological (human vulnerability as seen through the pandemic, migration and declining birth rates). The combination of these will create massive change in labour markets, and require a coherent response from employers, policy-makers, and others. Investors in particular have significant influence on businesses and markets.

Defining work

— We define work as a human response to God's creative work, and think of it not of creating but releasing value from a good creation. Work – including, but not limited to, paid employment – is the way human beings are connected to collective prosperity, to communities, and to meaning.

— Work as a 'response' is an important principle even for those who have a non-religious starting point. Human work should be underpinned with a kind of humility toward the limited resources we have inherited and marked by an attitude of stewardship for future generations.

— Work, however, often suffers from obvious tensions. Some experience aspects of their work almost as creativity and play; others exercise deep compassion through work. Some may articulate a sense of 'vocation' – that they specifically are drawn towards this or that particular work or purpose. For still others, work can be mentally, emotionally and financially unrewarding.

Humanising work

— Christian tradition recognises that, for the sake of the common good, work needs to be humanised. An excessive drive for profit from shareholders, and low prices from consumers, contributes to environmental and social harm. The labour share of income is declining in most western economies. As the growing number of people in in-work poverty shows, we have not solved basic problems around pay and conditions, and nor does the current settlement on in work benefits reflect needs.

— Technology and automation can be perceived as a threat. Rightly deployed, technology presents significant opportunities to humanise work. It can reduce the amount of time spent at work, and potentially keep and enhance the creative and fulfilling aspects of work. As a society, we do have a collective responsibility for those whose work has been displaced through automation if all are to be able to flourish. Employers in particular have a responsibility to help those whom they displace with technology to find new work, helping them re-skill if necessary. Such a response will broaden opportunity, and contribute to human flourishing. We want to see employers and the government/taxpayer contribute more to in work training, rather than assuming that individuals should bear the costs.

— A rebalance of power in the workplace is necessary if we are to see change on many of these issues, whether that comes through improved HR practices and wider consultation, or formal measures on worker representation.

Limiting work

A particular concern in the current context is the accelerating breakdown of boundaries between work and home life, driven by technological changes over time and now by the pandemic. The drive for flexibility has mainly been a benefit for employers, in particular through the assumption that workers will work overtime without pay. As well as tackling economic drivers of overwork, we should identify and institute shared practices of rest to help people to restore balance and boundaries.

Recommendations

— Our aim should be a 'full work' rather than 'full employment' economy. This may mean creating incentives for people to *move out* of the labour market for periods of time and for particular purposes that align with some public good.

— We need to make sure work genuinely pays, addressing ongoing issues through a new employment bill. Living wages, working conditions and benefits, and the ability to be provided for in retirement (including fair contributions to social insurance schemes through taxation) should be available to all workers. Minimum benefits ought to be available for all workers, regardless of their employment status.

— In order to help limit the intrusion of work into the rest of our lives, we need to change the culture of work in most work places. This could be encouraged by:

- Measures to tackle unpaid overtime – paying overtime would force employers to appropriately define job hours needed;
- More public holidays;
- Tackling unpredictable hours and low pay, which push people to take on multiple jobs, supporting Living Hours and Living Wage campaigns;
- An end to embedded surveillance in personal devices and at work more generally;
- Measures to establish a 'right to disconnect' from work after hours at a legislative level, and greater consultation with staff on working time at business level;
- Support 'fair trade' approaches to work such as Clean for Good.

Training and Education:

- Employers should bear responsibility to help those whom they displace to find new work, helping them re-skill if necessary;
- Companies and entire industries could also consider pooled training and qualifications either directly or through industry associations;
- All workers/citizens need training budgets with contributions from employers, government and individuals, which workers could draw upon throughout their working lives.

Meaning and Voice:
- We need to re-establish the voice of labour. Consultation with employees is to be applauded but should be universal. Giving an employee a say on how and when they work, and then taking that say into account in the outcomes gives employees a sense of having some control and influence over how they work;
- We all need to have a better understanding of our own consumption habits and their effects on labour. This could range from kite marks on products letting consumers know whether they were produced by people earning a living wage and working living hours to labels on electronic tills and ATMs itemizing the number of staff the machines have eliminated. A 'Trust Pilot' for the way employees are treated, or more generally around employers' attention to social issues might be one possibility;
- Encourage workplace chaplaincy and other forms of pastoral care for workers.
- Open up opportunities for workers to volunteer, adding volunteering hours to state social insurance worked hours credits.

- Investors should add clear requirements on the fair handling of wages, benefits, agency work, outsourcing and employee surveillance to the social criteria they look at within environmental, social and governance investing.

6 Introduction

On human work

In the winter of 1940/41, a young Polish poet found himself working in a limestone quarry as part of a Baudienst work crew. He later wrote verses reflecting on this period of forced labour. These respectfully reflected on how this heaviest of physical work was also mentally demanding.

> *No, not just hands drooping with the hammer's weight,*
> *not the taut torso, muscles shaping their own style,*
> *but thought informing his work,*
> *deep, knotted in wrinkles on his brow,*
> *and over his head, joined in a sharp arc, shoulders and veins vaulted.*

That young poet was Karol Wojtyla – later John Paul II. He is the only Pope in modern history to have worked as a manual labourer.

This experience coloured his encyclical, *Laborem Exercens*, published 40 years ago in September of 1981.[1] Published to coincide with the 90th anniversary of the first papal encyclical addressing "the social question", *Laborem Exercens* is a reflection on both the nature of work and its contemporary curses. Its central argument is that work has a dual quality: the objective (the different goals to which men and women could give themselves); and the subjective (what men and women become when they give themselves to those projects).[2] In other words, it proposes an existential understanding of work: work is not just what humans do, it is what they are. More theologically, work is humanity's imitation of the working creator God. Work, whether as paid employment or in another expression,

Work is as much a matter of our souls as our body.

does more than keep body and soul together. It gives a sense of meaning and purpose, and work is as much a matter of our souls as our body.

These types of claim risk sounding at best overly idealistic, and at worst sinister (like those corporate cultures that don't just want an employee's labour, but their inner life of joy and meaning). But the encyclical – alongside other traditions of Christian thought on work – also balances this idea that work is a vital part of our human identity with the idea that it is "cursed" in some way. "Cursed is the ground because of you; through painful toil you will eat food from it all the days of your life."[3] **When humans become alienated from creator, creation, and each other, then work becomes burdensome, difficult, and vulnerable to injustice and inequity.** Work is necessary and open to transcendence, but the sense of meaning, purpose, and transcendence will always be mixed with "painful toil". Any high view of work has to be accompanied by an analysis of how and why it often falls so short of ideals, and what can realistically be done to eliminate the worst abuses.

Laborem Exercens adopts Catholic Social Teaching's longstanding insistence that work needs to be *humanised.* As different forms of work emerge and recede, the challenges may appear in different guises, but they are usually the same in essence. There must be an ongoing and open-ended project to secure the priority of labour over capital (people before profit!), for workers to organise to secure rights, and to ensure that workers are paid a just wage.

The encyclical's reflection on technology is particularly pertinent to the current debate around work; it is "man's ally", perfecting, accelerating, and augmenting work. However, it can also

> *become almost his enemy, as when the mechanization of work "supplants" him, taking away all personal satisfaction and the incentive to creativity and responsibility, when it deprives many workers of their previous employment, or when, through exalting the machine, it reduces man to the status of its slave.*[4]

Prophecies about mass job losses through automation in the UK are probably unfounded, but technology could clearly be deployed in more or less humane ways.

This report seeks to consider contemporary issues around the status and future of work set within the framework of Christian thinking and practice. Western economies face a combination of factors which are changing or will change how we work: seismic technological change, the climate crisis, and the combination of demographic shifts and pandemic challenges. Economies and labour markets are always experiencing disruption, but as these three separate waves reinforce each other the result is a moment of unprecedented instability – and also of an opportunity to think about and do work differently. We could see the position of workers improve or deteriorate, but we will certainly see it change radically. This is not just an economic challenge, but a moral, social, and political one. It is also a spiritual challenge – to do with human meaning and purpose.

Faith in work

The existence of the *Laborem Exercens* reflects an historical interest in the nature of work throughout the Christian tradition. More than that, our economy and perceptions of work have been formed in different ways by different strands of Christian thought – perhaps most notably in Max Weber's thesis on the Protestant work ethic, which praises/blames Calvinist beliefs around self-discipline and frugality for the development of capitalism. Of course, many people disagree with this thesis. But however the currents of intellectual history have flowed, Christian thinkers and teachers have sought to understand work – not least because Christians have worked, and needed (and still need), to understand the meaning of work in relation to their spiritual life, beliefs, and practice. From early on, there was a (quite countercultural) sentiment that manual work was to be honoured. The Church Father John Chrysostom wrote:

> *Whensoever then thou seest one driving nails, smiting with a hammer, covered with soot, do not therefore hold him cheap, but rather for that reason admire him. Since even Peter girded himself, and handled the drag-net, and went fishing after the Resurrection of the Lord. And why say I Peter? For this same Paul himself, after his incessant runnings to and fro and all those vast miracles, standing in a tent-maker's shop, sewed hides together: while angels were reverencing him and demons trembling. And he was not ashamed to say, [Acts 20:34] "Unto my necessities, and to those who were with me, these hands ministered." What say I, that he was not ashamed? Yea, he gloried in this very thing.*[5]

The Christian tradition is not univocal on work – this much is apparent from St Paul's warning in one of his New Testament letters that people should continue working, in spite of whatever expectations they may have about the imminent return of Christ. Today, there are theological voices that have a high view of work (and employment – see below for the distinction) – John Paul II is indeed criticised for having too romantic a view.[6] There are equally voices that want to qualify the importance of work, suggesting that it is hopelessly trapped in an acquisitive framework that Jesus encouraged his disciples to reject. These sentiments have their secular counterparts. And outside of the space of intellectual/academic theological engagement there have been numerous faith-inspired movements that have sought to change work in some way. In the UK, we could cite the factory hours campaigns, famously paternalistic Quaker businesses, industrial chaplaincy, the worker priest movement, and the influence of Christianity on the trade union and wider labour movement. Again, the thrust of all this practical action has been to humanise, rather than revolutionise, work.

All these interventions addressed the challenges that came with industrialisation. We, however, face a series of new, distinct but interrelated, and pressing challenges. There is an urgent need to reassess work, and understand how it should be humanised today.

The technological wave

We are in the closing years of what some commentators have called the "de-industrial revolution" (the relative decline in the manufacturing sector in the UK, compared to other sectors in the country and compared to the manufacturing sectors in other economies).[7] The long tail of this de-industrialisation coincides with the beginning for the so-called "third" and "fourth" industrial revolutions – the growth of automated production, followed by the arrival of information

There is an urgent need to reassess work, and understand how it should be humanised today.

technology in all parts of the workplace, through to the emergence of "cyber-physical systems" (robots) and artificial intelligence (AI).

Some studies have claimed that around half of jobs are at high risk of automation. This is likely an exaggeration. In 2019, the Office for National Statistics (ONS) suggested that 7.4% of UK workers were at high risk of their jobs being automated, but 64.9% were at medium risk. Others contest the view that automation is a problem. A report from the Business, Energy and Industrial Strategy Select Committee recently argued that, "The problem for the UK labour market and our economy is not that we have too many robots in the workplace, but that we have too few."

The deeper issue might not be how many jobs are open to automation, but which. Automation may exacerbate the "hollowing out" of the labour market, where the relative proportion of mid-skilled

> **This hollowing out for the job market threatens the implicit social contract.**

jobs has declined compared to low- and high-skilled jobs.[8] Mid-level "routine" jobs are easily automated, whereas low-skilled (and low paid) jobs may not be worth automating and highly skilled complex work is not easily automated.[9] Since jobs that are more likely to be automated tend to be concentrated in certain areas, and are done by certain groups more than others (e.g., more by women than men), such a process will have an uneven influence across societies. This hollowing out for the job market threatens the implicit social contract.

The ecological wave

The second wave is the climate and ecological crisis. Ironically, it is the same economic progress and prosperity of the last 200 years that has caused this crisis, which in turn now threatens prosperity, along with human communities and the natural world. Large parts of western economies rely on artificially stimulating demand, supported by the availability of easy credit. This contributes to keeping the economy ticking, but at the cost of the wider flourishing of the planet and human race.

This is likely to move in (at least) two different ways. First, ecological change will directly affect some parts of the economy, challenging production or supply of goods and services. Some parts of the global economy already are directly and dramatically impacted by climate change. Researchers suggest, for instance, that crop yields have been adversely affected by changing weather patterns.[10] Second, a combination of shifting consumer demand and changing government regulation may increase demand for other types of products or services. Pressure from consumers, governments, and businesses themselves may encourage a "greening" of some parts of the economy, though whether this will be enough to mitigate ever-growing levels of consumption is open to debate. The International Labour Organisation observes that some jobs could be created, others eliminated, still others substituted – but that the majority of roles will be transformed in a changing climate.[11]

The anthropological wave

The COVID-19 pandemic saw radical change in how we work. On a macro level, there has been a step-change in how government has supported work, yet many jobs have disappeared, or may yet disappear. The number of payrolled employees is currently rising (June 2021). At 28.5 million, it is 553,000 below levels seen before the pandemic.[12] The gradual

withdrawal of furlough support could expose weaknesses in the jobs recovery.

Many will remember 2020/21 as the era of endless Zoom and Teams meetings, of a high level of work intensity (but no commute), and of seeking a new balance between work and home life. The reality is more complex. ONS data show that 54.3% of workers with a degree or higher qualification were doing some work from home in 2020, compared to 13.9% with no qualification. Rates of home-working were highest in wealthier boroughs of London. Even at the peak of lockdown, well below half of the national workforce (35.9%) were working from home. Data from the ONS suggest that men who worked in elementary occupations or caring, leisure, and other service occupations had the highest rates of death involving COVID-19. Rates were lowest in professional occupations.[13]

> **The deeper issue is not the pandemic but the brute fact of human vulnerability it symbolises.**

The deeper issue, from the point of view of work and employment, is not the pandemic but the brute fact of human vulnerability it symbolises. The global economy is experiencing such high levels of disruption because of a human illness. There are multiple other dimensions to this vulnerability. Hundreds of millions of people are likely to be displaced through the effects of climate change in the next few decades. The Brookings Institution estimates that one third of the 68.5 million people who were forcibly displaced in 2017 were forced to move by sudden onset weather events – flooding, forest fires after droughts, and intensified storms.[14] Other issues include falling fertility rates, which will reduce the amount of available labour and place stress on welfare systems.

Aims and methodology

The premise of this report is that these three waves together have changed and are changing the world of work. We are faced with new problems and new opportunities. Not only this, we have to establish a new way of thinking about these challenges – what has been called a "new conceptual basis".[15] The Christian tradition can be brought to bear to help us understand the nature and importance of work and how it can contribute to human flourishing in a different kind of landscape.

In it, we have drawn on three key sources.

1. **The wealth of Christian reflection on work and its place in human life.** Catholic Social Teaching (CST) is the clearest and most coherent, but by no means only, tradition of reflection and practice – though few general readers are aware of it. The foundations of modern CST were laid during the Second Industrial Revolution with the papal encyclical *Rerum Novarum*. More recently, significant documents include John Paul II's *Laborem Exercens* (briefly discussed above) and his *Centesimus Annus*, published in 1991, which also reflects at length on work ("By means of his work man commits himself, not only for his own sake but also for others and with others. Each person collaborates in the work of others and for their good. Man works in order to provide for the needs of his family, his community, his nation, and ultimately all humanity"). Pope Benedict XVI's *Caritas in Veritate* (2009) argues that the idea of "gift" should be as central to the economy and to the state as it is to civil society. Pope Francis' *Laudato Si'* focuses on environmental questions, but comments on work at length, arguing for the protection of work as the main route to human dignity.

2. **In January 2021 – at the height of the third UK lockdown – we commissioned YouGov to carry out polling.**[16] These questions focused on questions of work and identity. This data demonstrated quite a high level of dissatisfaction with work. Amongst a list of statements about work, 33% agreed that "work is just a way of earning to provide for life's necessities", compared to only 16% who agreed that "I feel that in work I'm doing things that are really meaningful", and just 10% who agreed that "I believe my current work is part of my calling and vocation". A significant number – 45% – said that they would retrain for a different career if they had the opportunity. However, ABC1 are far more likely to think their work is meaningful (21% of ABC1s think it's meaningful, compared to 10% of C2DEs).

There is a degree of concern around job security, though not always for the reasons that people expect. Only 18%, for instance, feared for their job role as a result of developments in technology (a higher 28% of 18- 24 years olds). However, 30% of respondents overall said that they "feel insecure about how long I will be able to hold on to my current job." At the time of the survey, around one in five workers said that they feared losing their jobs in the subsequent six months. When it came to the economy overall, and its likely impact on work, there was real pessimism – 85% were very or fairly concerned about the prospects for the UK economy.

3. **We held a series of three roundtables on the themes of a future of work**, drawing together thinkers and practitioners from businesses, labour organisations, the human resources profession, campaign and advocacy groups, academia, and the Church. These addressed

questions around (1) the goods of work, (2) humanising work, and (3) limiting work. Many of these participants to the roundtable (along with others) contributed scoping interviews to the project, helping us to identify and understand the key trends and challenges facing the world of work.

Each of these have informed the argument for this report in important ways, and we have of course drawn on the contributions of many others who are considering the future of work.

In the first chapter of this report we reflect on the nature of work, offering a theological definition of work as what humans do in response to the gift of creation. Work itself is fundamentally a human good – it connects us to shared prosperity, to different forms of community, and to purpose and meaning. Nevertheless, there is a tension between the goods of work, and work experienced as toil which we must attempt to resolve by seeking to humanise work. In the second chapter, we use this framework to identify some key ways in which we need to humanise work in our new context. In the third chapter, we argue that one of the unique features of the contemporary context is a loss of distinction between work and other parts of life, exacerbated by technology and the pandemic. We therefore make an extended case for better ways to establish boundaries and limit work.

For some years, there has been a vibrant public conversation about the future of work – it deserves nothing less, and we are far from the first to identify substantial challenges ahead. Though this project was planned before the COVID-19 pandemic, the consensus is that the pandemic has intensified and accelerated changes that were already taking place. A broad discussion, which touches not just on the economic, but the social, moral, political, and spiritual questions around work, is more timely than ever.

1 John Paul II, *Laborem Exercens* (The Holy See, 14 September 1981), www.vatican.va/content/john-paul-ii/en/encyclicals/documents/hf_jp-ii_enc_14091981_laborem-exercens.html. One of the problems with the encyclical is the unhelpful gender specific language, which we acknowledge will jar with many readers. However, we will quote without adjustment.

2 *Laborem Exercens*, §5 and 6.

3 Genesis 3:17b.

4 *Laborem Exercens*, §5.

5 John Chrysostom, Homily XX on 1 Corinthians 8:1, www.ccel.org/ccel/schaff/npnf112.iv.xxi.html

6 In reviewing a number of 20th-century theologies of work, John Hughes identifies Marie-Dominique Chenu as advancing an almost mystical view of work: "For Chenu, man in a 'collaborator in creation'... The Hegelian and pantheistic overtones are hard to miss... 'Man incorporates spirit in matter, according to his own nature, and, within the moving tide of history, creates the rock of eternity'." John Hughes, *The End of Work* (Oxford: Blackwell, 2007), p. 17.

7 In 1920 around 1.2 million people in the UK were employed in coal mines – in 2020 there were 2,000 (3% of the UK's 1920 population, down to 0.003% today). While there is disagreement around the causal factors and implications of this shift, most agree that capital has been directed too much towards short-term returns for shareholders rather than towards innovation. The result is that the UK economy is unbalanced geographically and that we have a large trade deficit.

8 Dr Steve McIntosh, "Hollowing out and the future of the labour market" (London: Department for Business, Innovation and Skills, 2013), https://assets.publishing.service.gov.uk/government/uploads/system/uploads/attachment_data/file/250206/bis-13-1213-hollowing-out-and-future-of-the-labour-market.pdf

9 Office for National Statistics, "Which occupations are at highest risk of being automated?" www.ons.gov.uk/employmentandlabourmarket/peopleinwork/employmentandemployeetypes/articles/whichoccupationsareathighestriskofbeingautomated/2019-03-25

10 Deepak Ray, "Climate change is affecting crop yields and reducing global food supplies", *The Conversation*, 9 July 2019, https://theconversation.com/climate-change-is-affecting-crop-yields-and-reducing-global-food-supplies-118897

11 International Labour Organisation, "Climate Change and Jobs", www.ilo.org/global/topics/green-jobs/areas-of-work/climate-change/lang--en/index.htm

12 Office for National Statistics, "Labour market overview, UK: June 2021", www.ons.gov.uk/employmentandlabourmarket/peopleinwork/employmentandemployeetypes/bulletins/uklabourmarket/june2021

13 Office for National Statistics, "Coronavirus (COVID-19) related deaths by occupation, England and Wales: deaths registered between 9 March and 28 December 2020", www.ons.gov.uk/peoplepopulationandcommunity/healthandsocialcare/causesofdeath/bulletins/coronaviruscovid19relateddeathsbyoccupationenglandandwales/deathsregisteredbetween9marchand28december2020#overview-of-coronavirus-related-deaths-by-occupation

14 John Podesta, "The climate crisis, migration, and refugees", 25 July 2019, www.brookings.edu/research/the-climate-crisis-migration-and-refugees/

15 Andrea Komlosy, *Work: The Last 1,000 Years* (London: Verso, 2018), p. 12.

16 All figures, unless otherwise stated, are from YouGov Plc. Total sample size was 3,182 adults. Fieldwork was undertaken between 5 and 18 January 2021. The survey was carried out online. The figures have been weighted and are representative of all English and Welsh adults (aged 18+).

1
What is Work?

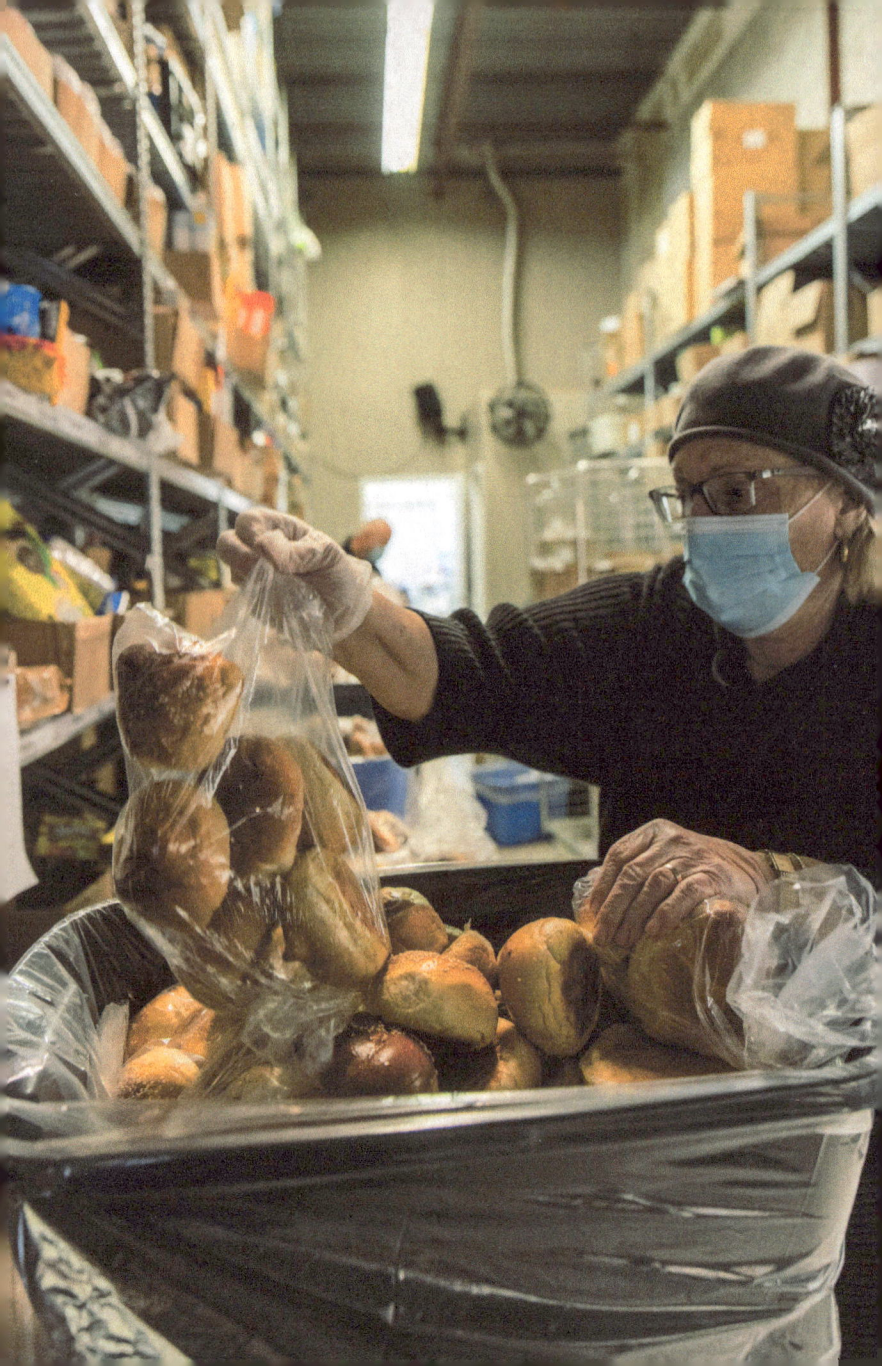

What it is we are talking about when we talk about "work"? It seems like a simple enough question; work is familiar and concrete, something many are engaged in every day. The more we think about work, the more difficult it is to define its essence. It's how we pay the bills, it's a place we go, and a task we do, but also somehow the core of our lives.

Statisticians, economists, and policy-makers tend to talk about "employment" – being paid to perform a task – rather than "work". However, employment is only one expression of work. For instance, in recent years, there has been increasing recognition of the prevalence and significance of unpaid work – particularly unpaid care work. In the UK and across the world, the majority of such work is undertaken by women. This in turn raises larger questions around gender equality and participation in the labour market, and indeed in terms of gender equality more generally. It also raises questions around the social recognition given to such work compared to paid employment, in spite of the fact that, although unpaid, such work has economic significance.

Understanding how work relates to employment is a key step in thinking about the issues. When we talk about "work" in this document we *are* usually talking about paid employment, which is how many if not most people experience work. However, we also need to be willing to root our thinking about employment in a deeper account. Work is more than the things we pay each other to do, and only by exploring its deeper meaning and wider goods – the ways it creates community, forms identity, and helps us forge meaning – will we do justice to its place in people's lives.

As societies change, both work and employment shift. There are diverse drivers of change – technological development, availability of resources (including labour), state regulation, social and religious norms. In fact, our contemporary idea of work primarily as employment – waged labour outside the home – only became dominant in the 20th century.[1] It is not clear that this emphasis on employment to the exclusion of other forms of work is helpful. Nor is it clear that it is immutable (as the greater recognition of unpaid care work indicates), especially at the convergence of the technological, ecological, and anthropological waves described above.

A theological contribution

Where could this deeper account come from?

"The annual labour of every nation is the fund which originally supplies it with all the necessaries and conveniences of life which it annually consumes," wrote Adam Smith in *The Wealth of Nations*.[2] Smith's account – and Marx's after him – treats work as foundational to human experience.

> **Our contemporary idea of work primarily as employment only became dominant in the 20th century**

It's understandable that an account of work must surely begin with the fact that labour is the way we sustain life, but a Christian perspective dissents from the idea that human work is "original". Most Christian ideas around work are "protological" – that is, concerned with origins – in that they begin with the theological polemic of the Genesis account. This means that human work isn't the first thing. Rather, humanity responds to something – something that comes to us as a gift. Both humanity and the created world have value before anything is done by or with them. They are, in biblical language, "good", and cumulatively "very good" from the start, and originally capable of sustaining humanity without cultivation.[3]

Human work is therefore a response to divine work, and human beings are made in the image of the divine worker.[4] Humanity does not *create* value, but it does *release* value – through the care, use, and enhancement (or, when it goes wrong, through destructive extraction) of goods inherent in what we have been given, and by cooperating – working with – other humans who have equally been given the gift of creation.

Even if it is somehow true that we receive creation as a gift, why is this relevant in political or economic terms? Against this challenge, we believe that if we want to create a labour market that enables true human flourishing, our starting point must go deeper than changeable political or economic realities which can themselves trap so many of us in harmful systems and patterns of behaviour. Through this lens, recognising work as a fundamentally responsive activity clarifies many of the best instincts we all feel about our working lives, and so helps us to understand what psychologically and socially might be happening in the world of work. After all, whether it's to the natural environment, or towards other human beings, work is indeed the way we respond to and interact with what is around us in order to realise value. Work links us to communities – colleagues, teams, organisations, and working traditions – and grounds us in citizenship, rooting us in societies and giving us a share in collective goals.

In this way, we quickly circle back towards the economic aspects of work: it is the means by which we tend to contribute to and benefit from collective prosperity (the common wealth)

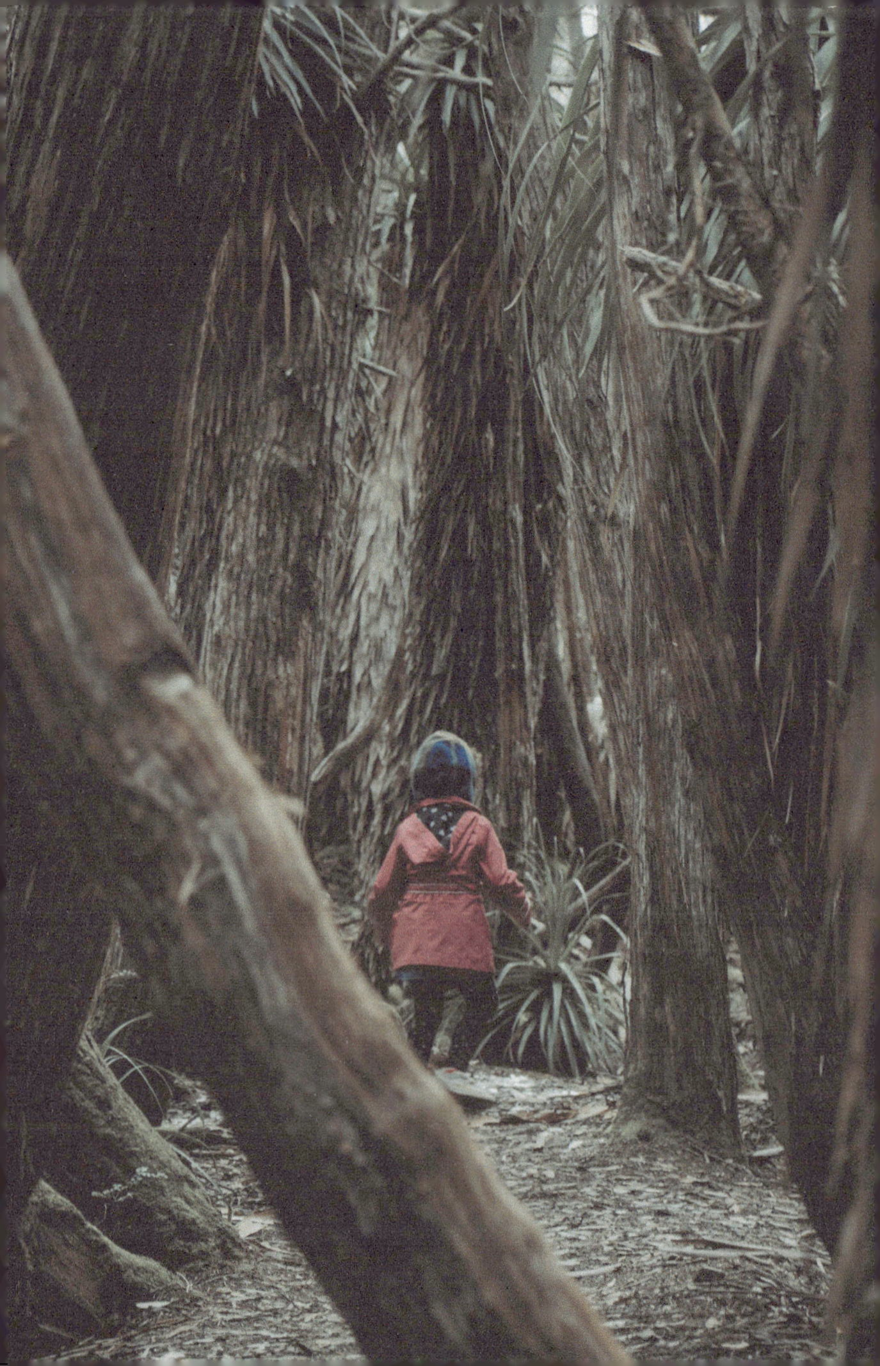

of the communities of which we are a part. But rather than reducing human beings only to their economic significance, right economy flows from right relationships.

This understanding of work as a "response" rings true whatever your moral starting point. Even on a purely secular basis, it is at least a happy accident that humans have evolved on a planet with the precise conditions for the flourishing of biological life and rich material resources. Even if there's no divine giver to whom we owe gratitude, then work and economic life as a whole should still be underpinned with a kind of humility – not least towards the limited resources we have inherited – and an attitude of stewardship for future generations.[5]

The problem of toil

However, have to ask why much of the work done today – paid or unpaid – is not experienced as a creative response to the richness of our material environment, but just as a thing necessary to sustain life. We really do work because we need to pay the bills (this was the most supported amongst a variety of statements we offered in our work survey – 33% agreed that "work is just a way of earning to provide for life's necessities").

> **Work and economic life as a whole should be underpinned with humility.**

This assumption fits with a view that – in economic terms – work is a *disutility*, a pain we have to endure for the gain of pay or reward. It has an opportunity cost, since during our work we can't do the things which we would prefer to be doing. Work is merely instrumental – a means to survive. Work may be more or less enjoyable, but that is incidental. We would avoid it if we could.

But this doesn't seem to be comprehensively true either. Our own polling suggests that for a substantial minority, work is about more than merely paying the bills. For example, 17% say that work is their way of giving something back to society. Substantial numbers are employed in the public sector (17.3% in quarter four of 2020)[6] or in other institutions that are oriented towards the public good such as charities. The National Health Service is one of the planet's largest employers. And of course, jobs in the private sector can also serve the common good, and the people that do them are similarly motivated by a range of things beyond personal gain.

There is, nevertheless, a tension in work. Many experience aspects of their work almost as creativity and play; others exercise deep compassion through work. Some may articulate a sense of "vocation" – that they specifically are drawn towards this or that particular work or purpose.[7] For still others, work can be unrewarding mentally, emotionally, and financially – a slightly less bad alternative to deeper poverty. Many of the most important in our society are both highly demanding and poorly paid.

How do we speak to this tension from our deeper account of work? Many thinkers have tried to separate work into a kind of hierarchy – Aristotle proposed *theōria* (contemplation), *praxis* (practical activity), *technē* (craft), and then slavery, each with less dignity than the one before. Hannah Arendt sought to separate labour from work, and both from action – only through the last of which we disclose ourselves as human beings. Christianity offers a simpler account. If all work is on some level a response to the richness of creation, then the work of a cleaner has just as much dignity as the work of a philosopher – but both will be on some level experienced with frustration, restlessness, and incompleteness. Alienation from

God, other people, and creation itself means that all work is experienced as "painful toil".

The goods of work

Work is both a joyful engagement with the gift of creation *and* painful labour for mere survival. It is intrinsically good, but under the discipline of extrinsic necessity. Work is human, and it is dehumanised.

Unveiling this tension has two implications.

The first is that work does have an inherent dignity. Its dignity comes before what we can achieve through it, but work is also the way we connect to shared prosperity, to community, and to a sense of meaning and identity. We open up these themes further in the rest of this chapter.

> **Work can be unrewarding mentally, emotionally, and financially.**

Second, work is a part of life that needs to be "redeemed" from toil and turned as far as we can towards human flourishing and the common good. This is the task of humanising work which we will address in Chapter 2.

Work as shared prosperity

Where does value come from? The standard economic answer is that it is created when the "factors of production" – land, labour, capital, and enterprise – are combined to produce goods or services which can be sold (others point to additional factors like intellectual or social capital). Since owners of land, capital, and entrepreneurs are relatively few, work and the wages workers receive are the main way that most people are connected to collective wealth.

Modern industrial relations have been largely a tug-of-war between labour and capital over the distribution of their combined productive value. The "labour share" is heading down in most developing economies, sometimes quite precipitously so, compared to returns to capital. In other words, work in the present system is not necessarily doing a very good job at distributing wealth. This heralds growing inequality (a Theos project on inequality is underway), frustration with elites, and political disruption.

> **Work is the way we connect to shared prosperity, to community, and to a sense of meaning and identity.**

A growing emphasis on long-term, sustainable growth considering the interests of all stakeholders should help re-open this debate. Additionally, if we can imagine a future where – at least in some industries – labour is not a significant factor of production, then this raises two profound social, political, and moral questions. First, how will people have an *income* on which to live? Second, but no less important, how can they continue to *contribute*? Their work contribution is often their stake in what Christian thinking calls the common good.

Work as community

The very language of economics hints at the way it is profoundly grounded in human relationships and collaboration: company, market – economics itself comes from the Greek word *oikos*, meaning "household". Work creates and sustains communities of different kinds. Catholic Social Teaching points out how integral work is to family, national, and global relationships, and with as well as communities across time:

> *The family is simultaneously a community made possible by work and the first school of work, within the home, for every person...*
>
> *[Society] is also a great historical and social incarnation of the work of all generations. All of this brings it about that man combines his deepest human identity with membership of a nation, and intends his work also to increase the common good developed together with his compatriots, thus realizing that in this way work serves to add to the heritage of the whole human family, of all the people living in the world.*[8]

Work is an opportunity for "love of neighbour", whether that neighbour is a fellow worker, team member, employer, manager or employee, customer, or even competitor. And indeed, this social element is especially underlined when we consider the structural importance of the workplace from a wider social cohesion perspective. Many job opportunities themselves come about as a result of social interaction (as many as four in ten jobs are filled through word of mouth), so that being economically active is itself a driver of further opportunity. Yet the workplace is also one of the main spheres of life where we connect with those who have different backgrounds from our own.[9]

The relational aspects of the workplace have been brought home during the pandemic. According to the ONS, 35.9% of the employed population did at least some work at home in 2020 (an increase of 9.4 percentage points compared with 2019). While this is not as high as might have been anticipated given the national lockdown, it may be that this marginal change will transform behaviour over the long term. Many individuals, teams, and companies may have crossed a threshold in the way they organise their work.

The nature of the workplace as a common endeavour expands beyond the (albeit immediate and very pressing) issue of post-COVID changes in work. How can the commonality of work be better reflected? Proposals have been made to add worker representatives to boards, or to develop German-style worker councils to give employees greater voice (the RSA suggests that these should be a condition of COVID support grants).[10] These proposals are a concrete way of reflecting the fact that a business and workplace are a set of overlapping interests – workers, managers, shareholders, and customers.

Work as identity and meaning

As we have argued above, we should think of work as a useful contribution to the common good as well as mere employment (in the pandemic we have seen how it's not just those in traditionally admired or highly remunerated professions that are significant for continuation of life in fairly extreme circumstances, but also those in roles that could be seen as mundane – truck drivers, shelf stackers, delivery drivers). This is an external or objective meaning – work for an important purpose. Without it, we can feel a sense of frustration in our work (though not as much as David Graeber suggested in his famous "bullshit jobs" thesis[11]).

Increasingly, work is also a place where we discover – depending on the right conditions – a sense of internal meaning. Ruth Yeoman, an academic specialising in ethics and practices of meaningfulness and mutuality in work, observes that:

> *It is needful also for us to satisfy our interests in having something worthwhile to do which is constituted by the goods or autonomy, freedom, and social recognition. The importance of such goods for shaping a person's life as a whole makes meaningful work a fundamental human need; that is, a need which is not to be met in any way whatsoever, but in a manner consistent with the kinds of creatures we are - beings who have unavoidable interest in being able to express free, autonomous action in association with others.*[12]

To describe meaningful work as a human need resonates with a Christian understanding which connects work to human purpose, and therefore as an aspect of each human being's development. This is John Paul II's "subjective" dimension of work. At least in this instance of Christian thought, this dimension is the *most important* dimension of work:

> *It only means that the primary basis of the value of work is man himself... however true it may be that man is destined for work and called to it, in the first place work is "for man" and not man "for work". Through this conclusion one rightly comes to recognize the pre-eminence of the subjective meaning of work over the objective one.*[13]

What does that signify concretely? Psychologically, there is of course a real form of meaning to be derived from simply doing a job – any job – well, and the feelings of competency and efficacy that arise from that. In the realm of values, it suggests that the well-being and development of workers should be a high priority, aligned with or ahead of profitability in importance. John Paul II in fact objects to the characterisation of labour as a factor of production – this fails to recognise the created dignity of human beings and the fact that they are the subject of work. It could also be reflected in the actual organisation of work, where workers can exercise some degree of autonomy and control at the level of individual tasks and at the level of the workplace overall. This extends the dignity we offer people in the social and civic realm into the workplace.

It is important to see that the discourse of meaningful work can be problematic. Unscrupulous employers can use workers' aspiration for purpose as a tool to leverage greater levels of psychological and emotional commitment, or to cynically "purpose-wash" business practices that are bad for people or planet. While the Christian tradition can affirm the idea that it is meaningful to talk about purpose and meaning, even worship, through work, it does so within clear limits. Not only can work become toil, as noted above, also, absolutely centrally, work springs from the gift of creation and is therefore rooted in rest and the biblical notion of Sabbath.

This is a question we will explore further in Chapter 3. Before this, however, we address more general issues around the humanisation of work.

1. Andrea Komlosy, *Work: The Last 1,000 Years* (London: Verso, 2018), p. 10.

2. Adam Smith, *The Wealth of Nations* (1776).

3. Genesis 1:10, 31.

4. Genesis 1.27.

5. Catholic Social Teaching proposes the idea of "the universal destination of goods". While things may be privately owned, "the original gift of the earth to the whole of mankind. The universal destination of goods remains primordial... Those who hold goods for use and consumption should use them with moderation, reserving the better part for guests, for the sick and the poor."

6. Office for National Statistics , "Public sector employment as % of total employment", www.ons.gov.uk/employmentandlabourmarket/peopleinwork/publicsectorpersonnel/timeseries/db36/pse

7. The concept is contested in the Christian tradition. The broadly Catholic position that only those called to religious orders or priestly ministry had a vocation, and the Reformer perspective that all Christians experience a calling to live faithfully in the domestic, church, and public spheres. Contemporary Catholic teaching readily extends to "secular vocations". For example: the laity, by their very vocation, seek the kingdom of God by engaging in temporal affairs and by ordering them according to the plan of God. They live in the world, that is, in each and in all of the secular professions and occupations. They live in the ordinary circumstances of family and social life, from which the very web of their existence is woven. They are called there by God that by exercising their proper function and led by the spirit of the gospel they may work for the sanctification of the world from within as a leaven. *Lumen Gentium*, Pope Paul VI, 1964, §31.

8. *Laborem Exercens*, §10.

9. Jon Yates, Fractured, 180. Social Integration Commission, *A Wake Up Call* (2014), pp. 12–13.

10. Alan Lockey and Fabian Wallace Stephens, *A blueprint for good work: Eight ideas for a new social contract* (RSA, 2020), p. 51, www.thersa.org/globalassets/reports/2020/a-new-blueprint-for-good-work.pdf

11. Bartelby, "Why the bullshit-jobs thesis may be, well, bullshit", *The Economist*, 5 June 2021, www.economist.com/business/2021/06/05/why-the-bullshit-jobs-thesis-may-be-well-bullshit

12. Ruth Yeoman, "Meaningful Work: A Philosophy of Work and the Politics of Meaningfulness", in Ian Geary and Adrian Pabst (eds.), *Blue Labour: Forging and New Politics* (London: IB Tauris, 2015), p. 184.

13. *Laborem Exercens*, §6.

2
Humanising Work

In the last chapter, we argued that the Christian tradition has much to say on the nature of work and its role in human flourishing. Work enables us to contribute to and benefit from collective human prosperity; creates community by connecting us to other people; and is one means by which we can live purposeful and meaningful lives. However, these are normative claims – claims that we know do not always reflect reality.

Christians have a long history of engagement with the world of work and have long sought to contribute to its humanisation. Because humans are created in the image of God, "we must emphasize and give prominence to the primacy of man in the production process, *the primacy of man over things*" (emphasis ours).[1] The economy exists for people, not people for the economy. Forgetting the order of this relationship leads to outcomes that range from: pay which is too low and expectations that are too high; poor working conditions; and effects on self-esteem and self-worth that lead to mental health problems. Dehumanisation in the workplace means we are left less connected to each other.

Our intention in the following chapter is to look at how we can restore a better balance between labour and capital in the face of both today's challenges and the consideration of work set out in earlier chapters. To do this, we will consider the current state of work by examining misaligned business objectives and their implications for pay and conditions, and benefits. We will then look at technology as both part of the problem and the solution, while also considering other interventions to humanise work such as opportunities for better training, and encouraging voice and agency in the workplace.

Misaligned business objectives

In order to maintain competitiveness, profitability, and growth, companies will tend to look to reduce the relative costs of their labour if they can. They might reduce benefits, outsource, or use agency workers. While it might not be impossible to combine shareholder interests with those of other stakeholders, there are well-publicised and recent examples of companies, such as Danone, pushed back from more sustainable approaches.[2] Some big-name start-ups are predicated on avoiding the cost of employment (i.e., by classifying their workers as self-employed). Public sector employers face a constant pressure to limit wage growth and numbers on the payroll, in order to keep a tight rein on public spending.

At the same time, consumers look to short-term horizons of convenience and affordability – the former due in part to the lack of spare time because of work demands. Globalisation has made the effect of their actions on individual workers invisible to them, making it hard to see the link between how they consume and the effect on wages and conditions until made aware by tragedies in the past, such as when a building full of workers making inexpensive clothing collapsed at Rana Plaza in Bangladesh. Domestically, the COVID-19 pandemic has drawn attention to the low pay and difficult conditions experienced by many essential workers.

When we look at efforts to humanise work below, it becomes clear that an improved understanding of the interlinkages and contradictions between many interests is a precondition of meaningful change. In many businesses and industries, a redistribution of some of the benefits towards labour will be necessary if we are to treat all workers with the dignity they deserve as humans – and so, in the end, dignified work involves a better sharing of the value created between labour and capital.

Pay and conditions

The 1981 papal encyclical *Laborem Exercens* reflects that:

> *Just remuneration for the work of an adult who is responsible for a family means remuneration which will suffice for establishing and properly maintaining a family and for providing security for its future.*

It goes on to say this "just renumeration" may include "*other social measures* such as family allowances or grants" (emphasis ours).[3]

When it was written, this encyclical was arguing that one person's salary should cover a family so that someone could stay at home to care for the family. These days, two earners are almost a necessity to cover the costs of a family, causing many single people to join forces to be able to afford a place to live, and making it especially difficult to manage as a single parent. All that follows should be read in this light.

The pandemic shift has made us rethink the social value of some occupations, especially relative to what they are paid. After all, the designation of "essential" workers is almost inversely correlated to pay. A report from The King's Fund notes that although pay for care workers has improved in recent years – £6.78 an hour in September 2012 to £7.89 in March 2018 with the introduction of the National Living Wage – their hourly rate is still below the basic rate of pay

> **The pandemic shift has made us rethink the social value of some occupations relative to what they are paid.**

in most UK supermarkets.[4] Care workers also face difficult working conditions, and their work often carries hidden costs (for transport, for instance). All work, especially that which looks to the needs of some of the most vulnerable members of society, ought to provide pay that eradicates in-work poverty, enabling the provision of food, shelter, and basic services for themselves and the dependents for whom they are responsible.

> **Low pay is often a symptom of deeper problems with business models.**

But 56% of those in poverty in the UK are in working homes.[5] Work remains a route out of poverty, but it is an increasingly tricky one.

The low pay problem is often a symptom of deeper problems with business models which ignore the value of the actual work being done. As an example, low pay in the care home sector is not merely a combination of constrained public spending and a cultural disregard for those doing this kind of work (though both of these are factors). Private care homes are increasingly in the hands of private equity investors, betting on guaranteed income from the public purse and an ageing population. Care homes have been passed from owner to owner in "leveraged buyouts", which load providers with unpayable debt (ultimately leading to the closure of homes).[6]

The complexity of the causality of issues like precarious work, gig work, and zero hours' contracts has implications for how we respond to them. Incompatible goals and power imbalances among stakeholders, as well as changes in the supply and demand for labour, drive the levers of change. Where most stakeholders can see advantage in change, compromise occurs. Better regulation and law may be needed when solutions to injustices cannot be negotiated.

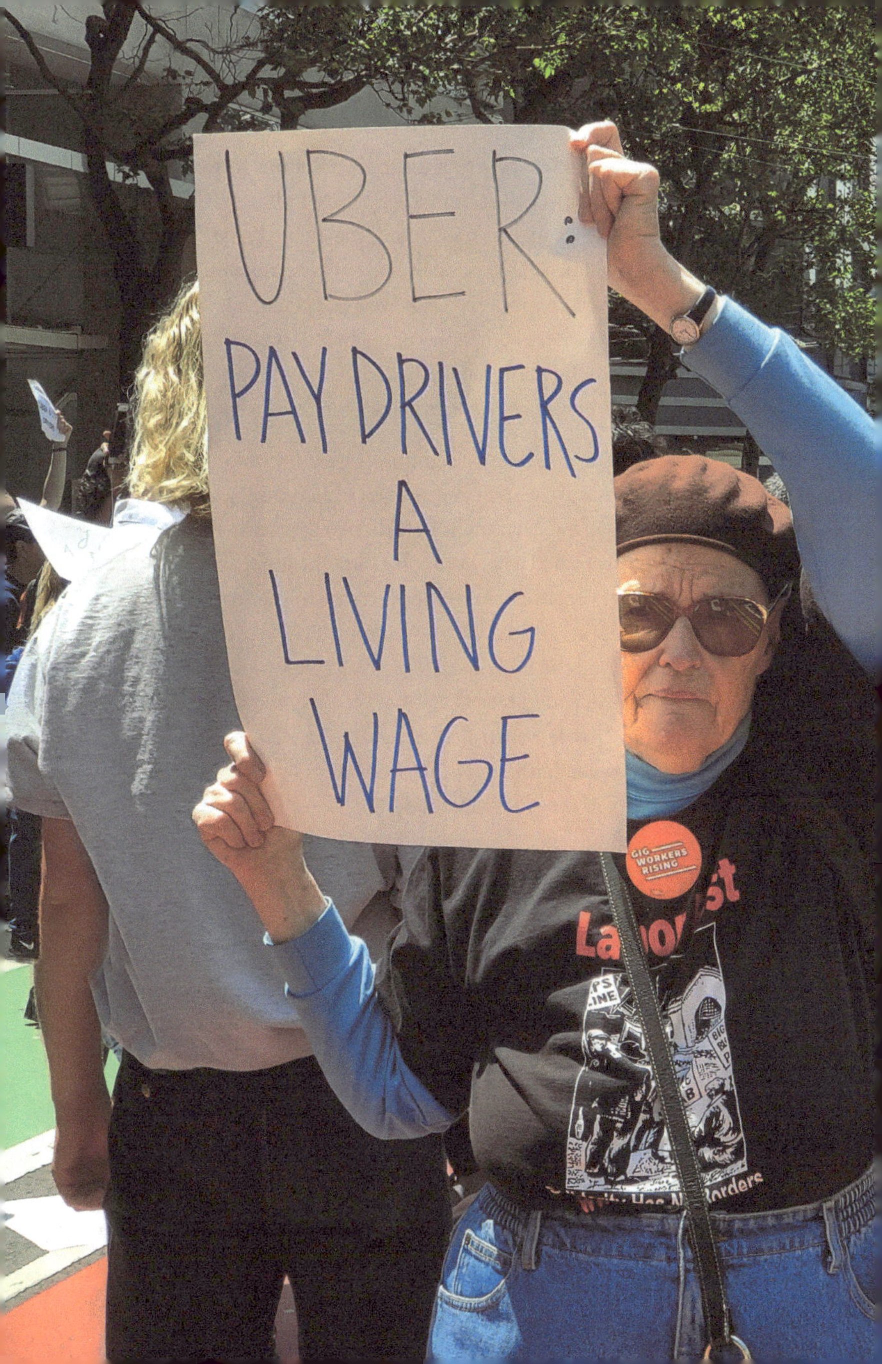
UBER:
PAY DRIVERS
A
LIVING
WAGE
GIG WORKERS RISING

The good news is that there are solutions to some of the misaligned incentives around pay and conditions. Grassroots campaigning, such as the work of the Living Wage Foundation (LWF), will be able to nudge some enlightened employers into better practice (and LWF has since begun a Living Hours Campaign where companies agree to four weeks' advance notice of scheduling, compensation for cancellation of hours, and a minimum of 16 hours a week for those who want it).

There is now also a significant need for union activity to further ensure worker representation as these new types of working grow. The Anglican Bishop of Oxford has campaigned for fair work in the gig economy, and the Independent Workers Union of Great Britain (IWGB) is trying to support the needs of gig workers. This year the Supreme Court ruled that Uber drivers had the right to be treated as employees instead of self-employed, and in May 2021 Uber officially recognised the GMB Union. This demonstrates that even platform economy jobs can be improved (although a question hangs over the long-term viability of the rideshare model).

Alternative "fair trade" approaches can help shift particular markets, or at least create fair trade alternatives. Companies like Clean for Good, a start-up created through a joint venture of London churches, are working to revalue the pay, condition, and treatment of office cleaners by developing a new business model. Other sectors may be so distorted that they require significant government intervention to resolve.

Benefits

In addition to problems with pay and hours, traditional employment used to offer a range of benefits: sick leave, holiday, compensation for in-work accidents, and pensions as part of the employment package. Many businesses have shifted responsibility for social costs from the employer to the employee, largely by making them "self-employed" instead of employees (see the case of Uber above), but also by trading benefits for pay to decrease long-term corporate liabilities. Also, state benefits are a hidden subsidy to employers in many cases, as National Insurance doesn't cover the costs in all cases. This has important knock-on costs for social insurance, sick leave, parental leave, holiday time, and pension savings.

The COVID-19 pandemic has taught us the dangers of a "work at all costs" culture that makes the workplace a vector for the transmission of illness when employees cannot afford to call in sick or self-isolate, worsened by the UK's Statutory Sick Pay being the lowest in Europe.[7] Sick pay has a meaningful impact in terms of outcomes for both workers and those they serve; care homes paying sick pay had fewer COVID-19 cases than those who did not.[7]

In addition, the Chancellor has indicated that the availability of furloughing for the self-employed during the pandemic is likely to be followed by an increase in social charges for the self-employed to cover these costs, making it even more difficult for these workers to make ends meet. In devising solutions to bring all workers to a minimum standard of living, we need to consider both pay, conditions, and benefits, but also fair contributions to social insurance schemes through taxation. Base minimums for benefits ought to be available for all workers, regardless of their employment status.

A 40-year shift from pensions that paid a percentage of an employee's final salary (defined benefit pensions) to a system where employers pay a fixed amount every month into an employee account (defined contribution pensions) has left much of the workforce and retired population with insufficient funds to provide for themselves in retirement. The creation of NEST, a workplace pensions scheme which makes a defined contribution plan available to any employee, is inadequate; employees who are not paid enough to meet their "ends of month" are in no position to supplement their employer's contribution, and employers' contributions alone are insufficient to fund retirement.

Can all benefit?

While decent pay and good working conditions may involve the reallocation of some profits from capital to labour in the short term, a longer-term, sustainable approach benefitting all stakeholders should result in lower staff turnover, lower training costs, and improved morale and trust that leads to higher productivity. Some benefits can be added, as of right, for all employees, regardless of their time in their job. Others, particularly those around pensions and skills, only work well where there is a long-term retention plan for staff. Where employee turnover is high and average tenure low, portable pensions and training budgets will make more sense.

Before we look at a few of the elements that can help create a humanised workplace, and in so doing help repair the fractured contract between employer and employee, it is important to look at the role of technology, which, in the wrong hands, is capable of further dehumanising work, but used well, can become an agent for positive change.

The role of technology

Technological change has shifted how we live and work throughout time. The plough dramatically increased the land one man could cultivate. In doing so, it displaced huge numbers of farmers. Automated manufacturing increased the supply and decreased the cost of goods, but led humans to service machines instead of the other way around. Today's information technology enables skilled tradesmen to focus on their work, while letting apps schedule their appointments, send out their bills, and organise their taxes.

The introduction of technology creates dislocations. First, those who it displaces are not always suited to the new work that technology creates, resulting in significant disruptions to both people and place as the nature and location of jobs shift. Second, decisions around new technology in the hands of the private sector are usually driven by productivity or profit considerations (where they are conscious at all – after all, the impact of new technology is often unknown or unpredictable). Recently, technology has also had a hand in the intensification of work, the "always on" culture and the creation of a surveillance culture, where employers use screenshots, mouse tracking software, video cameras, and call recording to ensure employees are working, and where artificial intelligence is used to monitor Uber drivers. It has revived the concept of piecework with apps like TaskRabbit, where gig workers are paid by the task. This both dehumanises the employee, and extends work into all aspects of our life.

Awareness of all these issues has increased during the pandemic, as working from home has brought these tools from our work environment to our personal space.[8] Not only does this feel more oppressive when brought into one's home, but there are real inefficiencies to such a culture. The need to be responsive to employer contact 24/7 means a poorer-quality leisure, and possibly poor concentration when working off-hours, leading to mistakes and worse performance during regular hours. These diminish all sense of responsibility and autonomy on the part of employees. Surveillance culture says clearly "we don't trust you", creating a culture of suspicion that works in both directions. Both can have a significant effect on employee mental health.

Moves to use technology to create a surveillance culture amongst workers must be stopped in their tracks. There is increasing discussion of the "right to disconnect", apps that automatically delete emails received during holiday time, and apps that will only send messages during office hours, discussed further in Chapter 3.

> **Moves to use technology to create a surveillance culture amongst workers must be stopped in their tracks.**

However, at the same time, real attention needs to be turned to what technology can do about toil. There have always been jobs that are unpleasant: from commercial dishwashing to cleaning sewers. But many such jobs are not well remunerated, so technology used to decrease costs rarely looks at such jobs first.

Rightly deployed, technology presents significant opportunities to humanise work. It can get rid of the drudgery aspects of people's jobs at the same time as enhancing productivity. It can reduce the amount of time spent at work, and potentially keep and enhance the creative and fulfilling aspects of work. In the care industry, a key example is the use of machines to monitor the health of the elderly so care workers can spend more of their time chatting with them. Many people could get rid of a significant portion of their work time spent doing unproductive, bureaucratic work (ranging from form filling to expense claims and time sheets) with the good use of technology, including the services available now for tradespeople mentioned above.

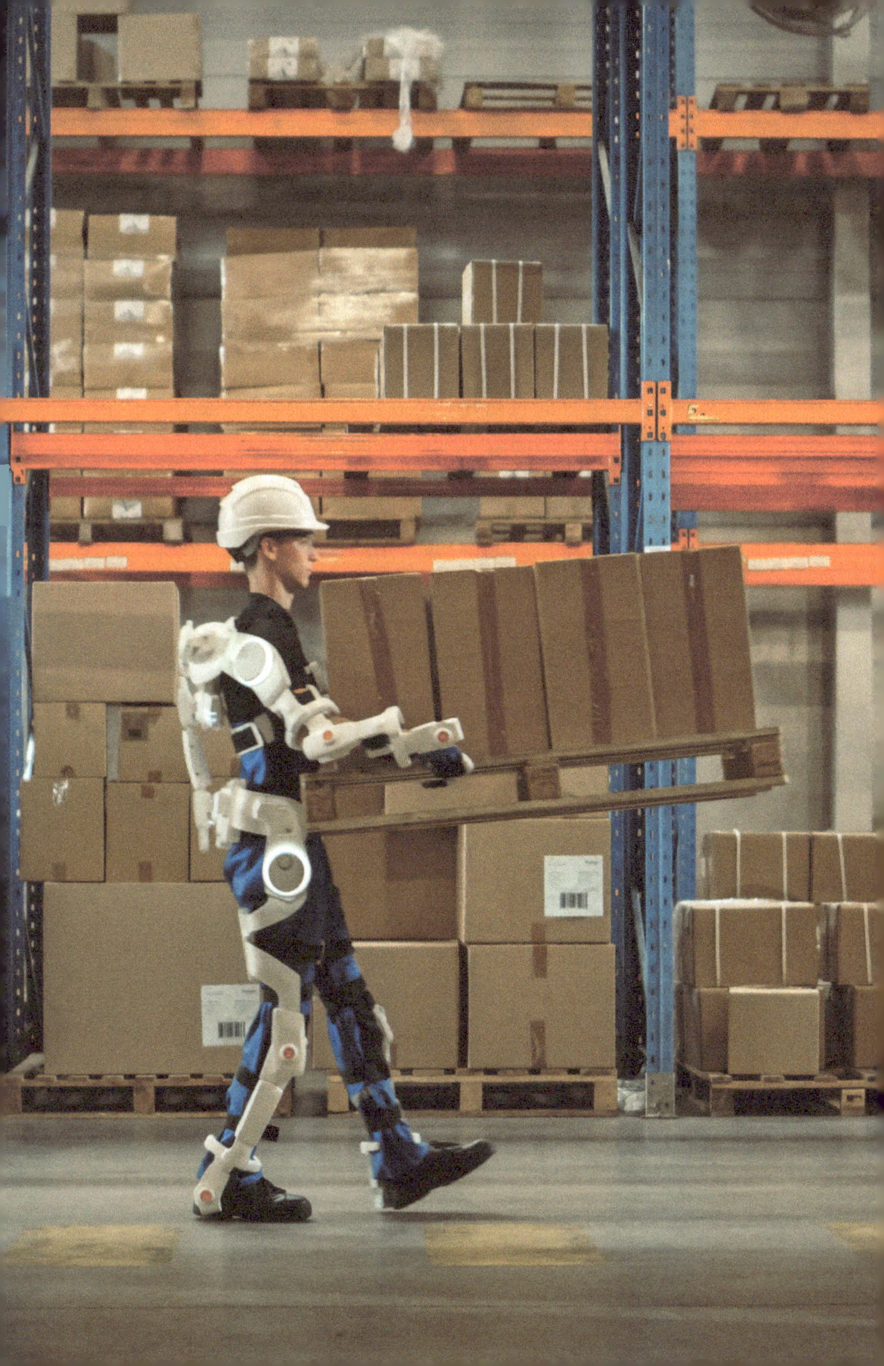

Deploying technology according to its potential to enhance human capacity, or decrease drudgery or monotonous tasks, could open up huge possibilities to improve working conditions, reduce working hours, and enhance the quality of both work and non-work time. If we look at agricultural work in the UK, it is currently dependent on migrant workers receiving poor pay and conditions. Automation and technology may permit a less seasonal, more stable, and more highly skilled, though likely smaller, workforce. To this end, the UK Department for Environment, Farming and Rural Affairs (DEFRA) announced in March of this year a Farming Transformation Fund to include grants for robotic and automated technology.[9] This is a direct attempt by government to encourage investment and innovation in automation and technology that supports a smaller, but more highly skilled, domestic workforce.

In a similar manner, technology used for good would enable older people to work longer, and reduce the physical damage inflicted by many professions. Artificial exoskeletons to help lifting for both builders and carers is just one example.

Whether automation is a humanising or dehumanising process will depend much on the social, economic, and business context. It has been observed that the problem in the UK economy is not that we have too many robots but too few, and that automation can improve productivity and quality of work. As a society, we do have a collective responsibility for those whose work has been displaced through automation if all are to be able to flourish. Employers in particular have a responsibility to help those whom they displace with technology to find new work, helping them reskill if necessary. Our polling indicates that 45% of all workers in England and Wales would be keen to retrain, with this number rising to 53%

amongst 18 to 24-year-old workers. Provided they are properly supported, many workers are open to the prospect of change. The key is to ensure that quality work remains available.

Training and education

For years, corporations have shifted training responsibilities to staff and qualifications providers to cut costs. In the 2021 Queen's Speech employees were encouraged to borrow to improve their skills, further shifting responsibilities from employers to workers, while other countries are much more proactive in their approach.[10] As technology displaces some workers, from self-pay tills and e-commerce in retail to automation in manufacturing or support staff, business has been replacing labour with technology but taking little or no responsibility for the unemployed and unskilled they leave in their wake. Rather, they expect government to pick up the cost of reskilling and retraining, all the while complaining that schools and universities are not producing employees with the qualifications they need.

It is time that business takes greater responsibility for the necessary retraining and reskilling, especially as shareholders have collected most of the benefits to date of these shifts. Business needs to train both the people they let go and the people they retain if they want labour force skills to reflect their needs.

> **It is time that business takes greater responsibility for the necessary retraining and reskilling.**

The first of the possible options is for employers to provide money for departing employees with good ideas for either start-ups or retraining. Second, companies and entire industries could also consider pooled training and qualifications either directly or through industry associations, which already exist in many industries such as finance, banking, and investment management. Such training is usually based on increasing skills and achieving qualifications, but is too often oriented towards the skill needs of the past instead of the forward-looking skills that will be needed for the future. Third, everyone needs training budgets with contributions from employers, government, and individuals, which workers could draw upon throughout their working lives. Current government proposals for "borrowing to train" schemes are ineffective for older staff wanting to retrain, as they may not be able to get sufficient return on training for their residual working life that makes borrowing for the full cost effective. The nature of changing technology and science both suggest that all workers will need successive retraining over the course of their working lives to adapt.

Training and retraining work best where interest and aptitude meet, including attention to soft skills when deciding on a course of training for someone. This will decrease frustration and be more likely to provide alternative work that the person finds satisfying. For example, the aptitude of retail staff for being retrained as care workers depends largely on whether what they like about retail work is a function of the people skills or some other aptitude.

A learning culture that helps all people recognise that the skills they will need to master will change over the course of their lives begins in primary and secondary education by teaching students *how* to learn and how to teach themselves. Too often graduates think of themselves as "done with school" when they will need to be learning throughout their lives.

Making this clear is necessary before any overhaul of the adult education system can be successful. Nonetheless, the idea that all citizens should be regularly picking up new skills, whether for work or pleasure, is one that should be fostered.

In addition to direct training, volunteering is one way some people can acquire new skills and enhance future employment prospects. When misused, the result is the unpaid internship schemes that abound, and are often prerequisites for graduates to get a foot in the door. Genuine volunteering – meeting a need from the charitable sector – should be defined as distinct from internships, which should be term-limited positions for which a living wage is paid.[11]

For the purpose-based business, this kind of skilling becomes part of their social contribution. When "jobs for life" are gone for good, the combined employer-employee responsibility to prepare the work force for their next job is vital.

Voice and agency in the workplace

Building on the discussion of Ruth Yeoman's work on meaning in Chapter 2 (see p. 46), almost every job, *correctly structured*, makes the doer feel they are making a contribution and gives them both a sense of participation and dignity. Sadly, outsourcing and the breaking up of jobs that use a range of skills into tasks that require little, if any, interaction or complementarity of skills decrease this sense of responsibility and human agency.

The pandemic has made us rethink the value of presenteeism and productivity at work, versus a more flexible mix of home- and office-working for those whose occupations permit it. Those happy and more productive when they work from home could be benefitting from a sense of both more autonomy and more control. They get to mix work with family and leisure in a way that rigid hours and a long commute did not permit, incorporating more non-work activities in their days without necessarily losing work productivity.

However, those with poor home environments have often suffered during this period due to a sense of loneliness and isolation, reflecting a recognition of the need for relationship and community. In this way, home-working has in some cases made explicit what employers have been able to ignore before this point: that our work lives are not just separate from the rest of us, but can generally be easier to navigate when the whole of life is happier.

Until recently, many would have looked to the labour movement to stand up for the rights of employees. However, after one hundred years of progress, the labour movement has been hugely diminished in its ability to support workers since the 1980s, as evidenced by significant declines in membership since 1979, reaching an historical low of 6.2 million in 2015–16.[12] It is encouraging to find membership increasing slightly in the last three years. Some of this was due to conscious intent on the part of business and government, and some due to the rapidly changing nature of both union membership and work itself. However, the pendulum has now swung so far away from worker power that there is an argument for a need to re-establish the voice of labour. In particular, the pandemic saw a return to the use of the concept of "solidarity", where each of us bears some responsibility for the condition of all of us.

Without the countervailing pressures of labour organisations, it will be difficult to encourage the changes proposed here. It is increasingly likely that pressure on business to change will come from not only unions, but also from investors increasingly concerned with the social aspects of environmental, social, and governance investing, and from governments where voters demand such attention. As mentioned above, all stakeholders will need to engage in solutions given the complexity of the causal factors.

So how do we increase the voice and agency of workers?

> **Without the countervailing pressures of labour organisations, it will be difficult to encourage change.**

— First, the pandemic has shifted the concept of presenteeism dramatically and many businesses are rethinking how often employees need to be in the office, albeit in part to shift the cost of premises from employer to employee. Many employers are consulting with employees on how they want to work in future before making decisions. **Consultation with employees is to be applauded but should be universal.** Giving an employee a say on how and when they work, and then taking that say into account in the outcomes gives employees a sense of having some control and influence over how they work. As noted in Chapter 1, worker presence on boards, and German-style worker councils, are some ways this input can be ensured in practice.

— Second, **we all need to have a better understanding of our own consumption habits and their effects on labour.** This could range from kite marks on products letting consumers know whether they were produced by people earning a living wage and working living hours to labels on electronic tills and ATMs itemising the number of staff the machines have eliminated. A "Trust Pilot" for the way employees are treated, or more generally around employers' attention to social issues might be one possibility.

— Third, **unions themselves need to rethink their structures, hierarchies, motivations, recruitment, and direct-action techniques to reflect a changing workforce and society.** They need to consider how they can best represent not only the interests of their members, but the interests of the wider workforce, both present and future. The full extent of how this can be accomplished is beyond the scope of this report, but without genuine, high-quality representation of all workers, most of the other recommendations in this report will not occur.

Towards more humanised work

We need to be both specific in tackling the problems at hand, but cognisant that, at some level, different working terms and conditions may suit different people at different times in the course of their working life. As just one example, for those studying or with caring responsibilities or just other interests, gig work can permit a source of income and satisfaction on a part-time basis. However, for other gig workers dependent on these wages for supporting a family, insufficient pay and a lack of security to plan and care for themselves and their families is a tragedy.

For this reason, the countervailing pressures of labour organisations, government regulation, and good business practice must set baseline conditions to enable everyone who wants to contribute to a good work society to be able to

Free Cash
withdrawals

do so. This means **the establishment of living wages and benefits, the ability to be provided for in retirement, and the opportunity to acquire skills and training** necessary to finding and keeping good work over the course of their working lives.

Workplace chaplaincy can also make an important contribution. Workplace chaplains provide pastoral care including a safe space for staff to voice their concerns and uncertainties as well as their hopes. Moreover, they can also be a safe conduit for workers' concerns that they hear regularly and support employers' efforts to resolve them. Their concerns lie entirely with the people at work, giving them both insights and perspective that others lack.[14] A chaplain has little interest in the employees' performance or the company bottom line.

Work will always be a place people search for meaning, belonging, and identity, even if it should never be the only place. Temporary, agency, and precarious work make this difficult. But we have seen how much can be done to make jobs less alienating and look less like toil. The next chapter will consider how to find ways to put work back into proportion with the rest of our lives.

Humanising Work

1 *Laborem Exercens*, §12.

2 Arturo Bris, "Danone's CEO has been ousted for being progressive – blame society not activist shareholders", *The Conversation*, 19 March 2021, theconversation.com/danones-ceo-has-been-ousted-for-being-progressive-blame-society-not-activist-shareholders-157383#:~:text=Danone's%20chief%20 executive%20and%20chairman,the%20board%20find%20a%20replacement

3 *Laborem Exercens*, §19.

4 Deborah Ward, "Average pay for care workers: is it a supermarket sweep?", King's Fund, 30 August 2019, www.kingsfund.org.uk/blog/2019/08/average-pay-for-care-workers

5 Andrea Barry, UK Poverty 2019/20: Work, Joseph Rowntree Foundation, 7 February 2020, www.jrf.org.uk/report/uk-poverty-2019-20-work

6 Vivek Kotecha, "Plugging the leaks in the UK care home industry", Centre for Health in the Public Interest, November 2019, www.chpi.org.uk/papers/reports/plugging-the-leaks-in-the-uk-care-home-industry/

7 OECD, "Paid sick leave to protect income, health and jobs through the COVID-19 crisis", 2 July 2020, www.oecd.org/coronavirus/policy-responses/paid-sick-leave-to-protect-income-health-and-jobs-through-the-covid-19-crisis-a9e1a154/

8 Office for National Statistic, "Impact of coronavirus in care homes in England", Office for National Statistics, 3 July 2020, www.ons.gov.uk/peoplepopulationandcommunity/healthandsocialcare/conditionsanddiseases/articles/impactofcoronavirusincarehomesinenglandvivaldi/26mayto19june2020

9 Alex Christian, "Bosses started spying on remote workers. Now they're fighting back", Wired, 10 August 2020, www.wired.co.uk/article/work-from-home-surveillance-software

10 Gordon Jones, "The Farming Investment Fund: An Overview", Department for Food, Environment and Rural Affairs, www.defrafarming.blog.gov.uk/2021/03/30/the-farming-investment-fund-an-overview/

11 Fabian Wallace-Stephens and Emma Morgante, "Who is at Risk? Work and Automation in the Time of Covid-19", RSA, 2020, p. 51. Authors note that "for every year a person works full-time in France, they now receive €500 worth of training credits, up to a maximum allowance of €5,000. While as part of Singapore's SkillsFuture program, all adults over 25 now receive S$500 (£280) in training credits each year. As in France, these credits can be stockpiled and drawn down across a person's working life. Once accrued by workers they are retained if they move jobs or become unemployed." www.thersa.org/globalassets/_foundation/new-site-blocks-and-images/reports/2020/10/work_and_automation_in_time_of_covid_report.pdf

12 Andy Haldane, "In giving, how much do we receive? The social value of volunteering", A Pro Bono Economics lecture to the Society of Business Economists, London, 9 September 2014, www.bankofengland.co.uk/-/media/boe/files/speech/2014/in-giving-how-much-do-we-receive-the-social-value-of-volunteering.pdf?la=en&hash=7212BE90FDC43B593224B854AA66FCBC5BD3B3AD

13 Alexandra Topping, "Union membership has plunged to an all-time low, says DBEIS", *The Guardian*, 1 June 2017, www.theguardian.com/politics/2017/jun/01/union-membership-has-plunged-to-an-all-time-low-says-ons

14 Our recent chaplaincy report, which makes exactly this point in regard to the importance of chaplaincy and homeworking. pp. 13, 85–86, 95, 102, www.theosthinktank.co.uk/cmsfiles/Relationships-Presence-and-Hope.pdf

3
Limiting Work

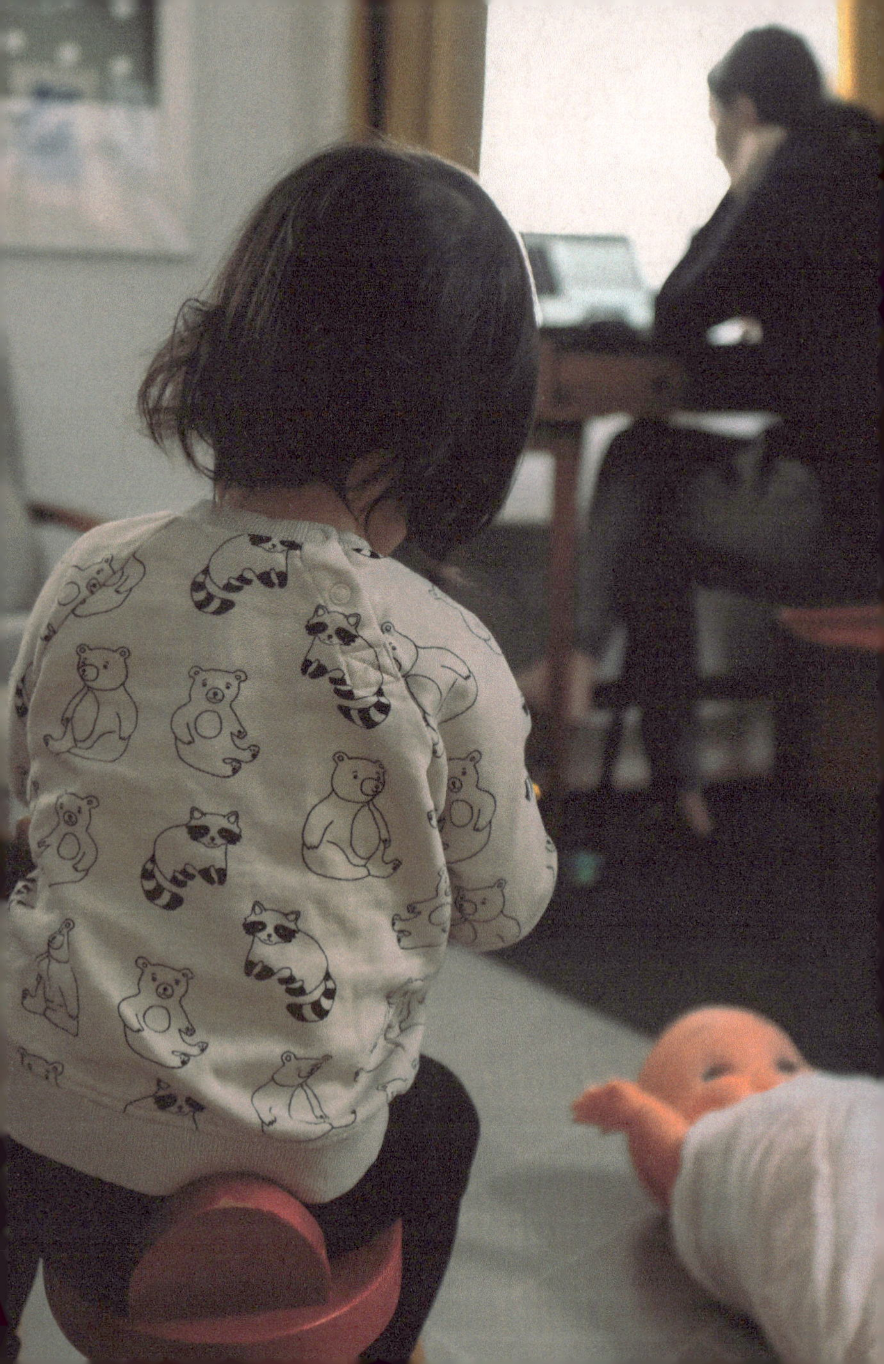

The economist JM Keynes believed that we would arrive at a four-hour working day by the end of the 20th century while still earning enough to meet all basic human needs.[1] He miscalculated in at least two ways. Keynes underestimated the ability of greed and covetousness to increase people's wants of not just goods but services and experiences that would impel them to spend more time working for money. He also misunderstood that while new technology and productivity gains reduce the time it takes to do things, they in turn create wholly new work and occupations.

Today we face a new problem in the world of work. It's about the time and space in which work occurs, and the implications of a potential shift from workers sharing physical space to sharing online space (whether working from home, or working through an online platform in the gig economy). For many, work is no longer a matter of going to a workplace, but of giving sustained attention to a particular task.

Through the pandemic experience we have learned about the negative effects of the loss of boundaries between our work life and the rest of our life, and the importance of other aspects of our life such as family and community. The result is paradoxical. Some experience greater freedom in work because of the ease of putting it down and engaging in other activities. Others find difficulty in stopping attending to work, and in attending to other things. Meanwhile, managers and employers will be anxious to ensure that they are getting their employees' attention. These problems arise as the boundaries between

> **Through the pandemic we have learned about the negative effects of the loss of boundaries between our work and the rest of our lives.**

work and other areas of life have dissolved, and will likely characterise work in years to come.

What has happened to our working hours?

Working hours are, by most measures, down over time, and on paper, the situation for workers appears to be improving. The on-the-ground situation, however, looks markedly different, for two key reasons.

First, though *official* UK working hours are down, a combination of unpaid overtime, performance pressure at work, and the need of the self-employed to be constantly on the lookout for work mean many people are working longer hours than ever. The UK would have been on target to reach a 30-hour week (equivalent to a four-day week relative to 2016) by 2040 had average hours continued to fall after 1980 in line with the initial post-war trend, where the average full-time week in the UK fell steadily from 46 hours in 1946 to 40 hours by 1979. From 1980 onwards, however, this trend faltered following labour market deregulation, and reduced collective bargaining; so that the average full-time week fell by just 2.5 hours to an average of 37.5 hours by 2016.[2] Moreover, those with uncertain work need to be constantly on the lookout for available hours. While the hours in paid work may have declined, the time spent looking for work and worrying about finding that work have increased.

Second, over the last few decades companies across the UK have reduced or removed payments for unsocial hours and overtime working. The rise in the number of workers having to do unpaid overtime has resulted in the erosion of the idea of the "standard" working day in the UK.[3] This leaves us where we are now: in the past three quarters, 17% of UK workers have worked more than 45 hours per week.[4] The Trades Union

Congress believes this unpaid overtime is worth £35 billion per year, and is equivalent to £6,828 per worker being taken out of pay packets.[5] The recent British Gas dispute was in essence around overtime pay.[6] A parliamentary committee report on Workforce Burnout and Resilience in the NHS and Social Care recently recorded that:

> ...discretionary effort is the rocket fuel that powers the NHS... If staff worked to contract and worked to rule, we simply would not be able to provide anything like the quality of care that is needed. Part of the problem is that we are relying relentlessly on the good will of our staff.[7]

Flexibility – but who benefits?

This goes partway to explaining why UK workers in theory enjoy historically low working hours, and compare not unfavourably with similar economies, but report feeling overworked, unrested, and say that their mental health is suffering. For the sake of flexibility, we have sacrificed clear boundaries between work and non-work. This has been a long process, intensifying in the knowledge economy from the turn of the century, and now made worse by the pandemic and working from home. Those working from home have had to negotiate a changed intensity of work, or even increased surveillance. Have we been working from home, or sleeping in the (new) office? This now negatively affects people in all parts of the labour market, though in different ways. Some will be asked to put surveillance apps on their own devices, while others, like Amazon drivers, will effectively work under permanent surveillance. Amazon is testing an "always on"

> **Have we been working from home, or sleeping in the office?**

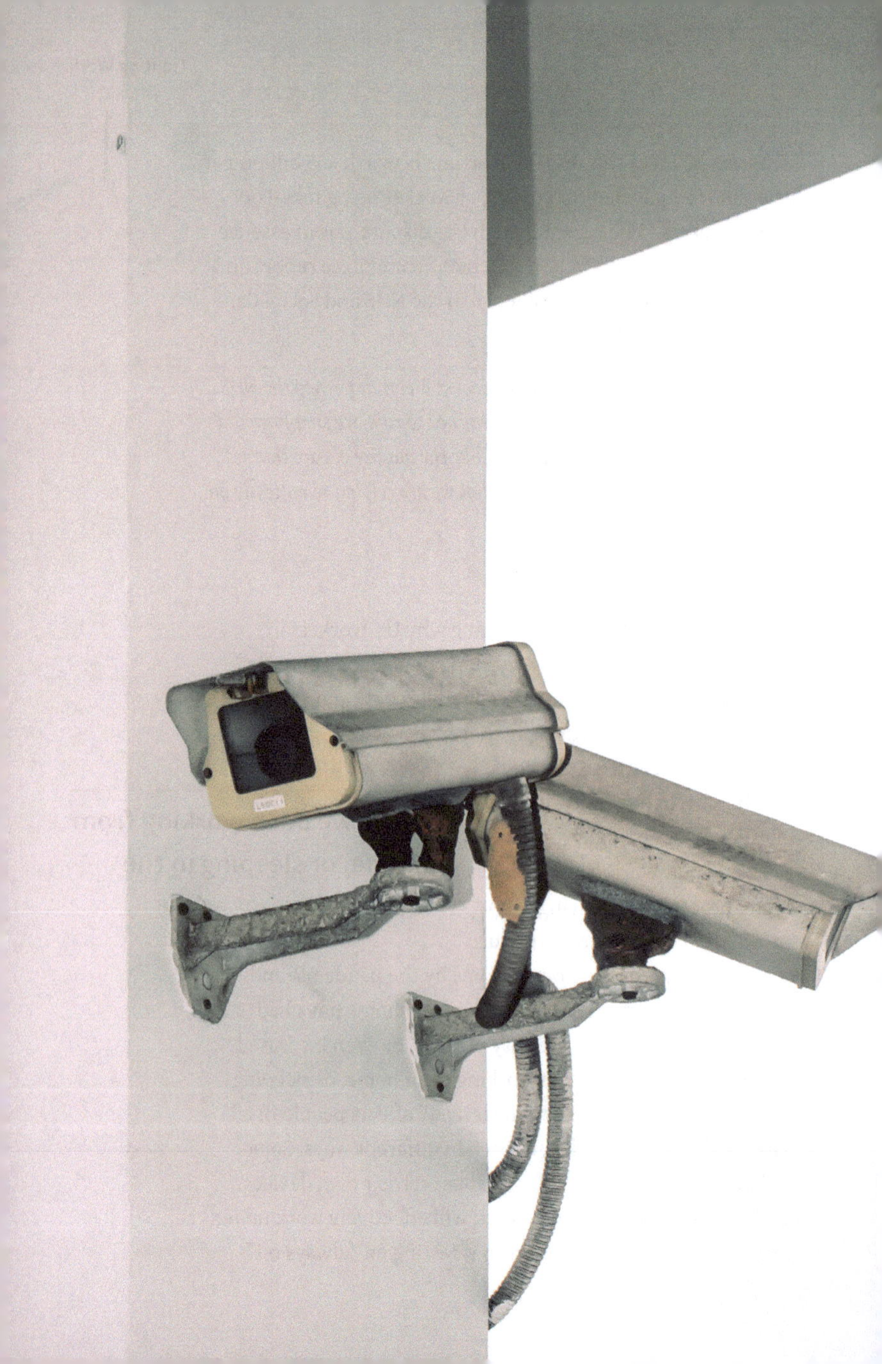

four-camera system in its delivery vehicles that monitors a driver's every move.[8]

Monitoring is not new. People have been punching time clocks since the dawn of the industrial age. However, now the technology is more invasive and insidious, and the line between good for the worker and good for the employer can be blurred. At PWC, a major accounting firm, partners are given Fitbits so long as they permit the data on them to be available to their employer. While this may alert the company to overwork and work-based stress, it is a landmark invasion of privacy.[9]

Some of the loss of hard work-non-work boundaries was a result of fear of demotion or dismissal during periods of abundant labour supply. Many workers lacked the power to say "no". Over time the encroachment of work into all aspects of our life became ingrained in the performance culture. This in turn created a chicken and egg problem; as work came to take so much of our time, many people struggled to find meaning elsewhere in their lives and worked more.

The cynical will argue that increasingly defining ourselves in terms of our work plays into the hands of our employers. Pre-pandemic, "cool" workspaces prided themselves on football tables and evening drinks on the premises, so that staff didn't even have to leave work for entertainment. High-pressure environments like Bloomberg give food, snacks, dry cleaning, and concierge services to ensure that employees have no distractions. This tendency may actually increase further post-pandemic in an effort to lure key staff back to their offices.

As Madeleine Bunting writes:

> *A work ethic has evolved that promotes a particular sense of self and identity which meshes neatly with the needs of market capitalism, through consumption and through work. Put at its simplest narcissism and capitalism are mutually reinforcing.*[10]

Defining ourselves by what we do instead of who we are – "I am a plumber; I am a teacher" – has been true since people took last names from their professions in the Middle Ages such as Cooper, Smith, or Thatcher. Still, the pressure to give all to work, if only to own more stuff, seems to have grown over time. To the extent we get time away from work, it is filled with care responsibilities, life admin, and the rest needed to make us fit for our jobs on the next shift. Work has become so dominant in our culture that rest or leisure is increasingly only a means to serve work.[11]

Recovering Sabbath

> *Remember the Sabbath day, and keep it holy. Six days you shall labour and do all your work. But the seventh day is a Sabbath to the LORD your God; you shall not do any work—you, your son or your daughter, your male or female slave, your livestock, or the alien resident in your towns. For in six days the LORD made heaven and earth, the sea, and all that is in them, but rested the seventh day and consecrated it. (Exodus 20:8-11)*

> **In the Judeo-Christian tradition, we are commanded to rest as God rested in celebration of his creation.**

Is it the loss of respect for the Sabbath that has led us to our emphasis on work, or is it our emphasis on a 24/7-work culture that has led us to abandon the Sabbath? Whatever the causality, this section examines the culture of the Sabbath and what we can learn from it.

In the Judeo-Christian tradition, we are commanded to rest as God rested in celebration of his creation. This religious prohibition to work on a Sabbath far outlasted those on lending at interest (and still holds in some countries today – Germany, for instance).

There is no doubt that it became associated with a harsh moralism, and that proponents of Sunday trading were more successful in persuading the public that liberalisation was in their interests. Nonetheless, the Sabbath day as a common rest day was what the philosopher Matthew Crawford calls a "cultural jig" – an embedded social practice which instituted a norm or public good, albeit by limiting choice and freedom of action.[12] It's true that, once removed, many of us experience greater freedom of choice. Yet this freedom has come with a downside: not only are many required to work on their Sabbath, but the sense of balance in our lives, our families, and our mental health all suffer.

Sabbath enforces "that the earth is a gift of divine creativity, given to humankind in sacred trust."[13] It emphasises that all of what we are and what we have exists as a gift. How we respond to that gift is critical. In this way, it reminds us that our lives are less about accomplishment but acceptance; less about achievement than gracious receipt of what we are given.[14]

This logic of gift should lead us to ask different questions:

not only "What do I want from life?" but also "What does life want from me" and "What does God want from me?" These questions remove us from the centre of our lives and create room

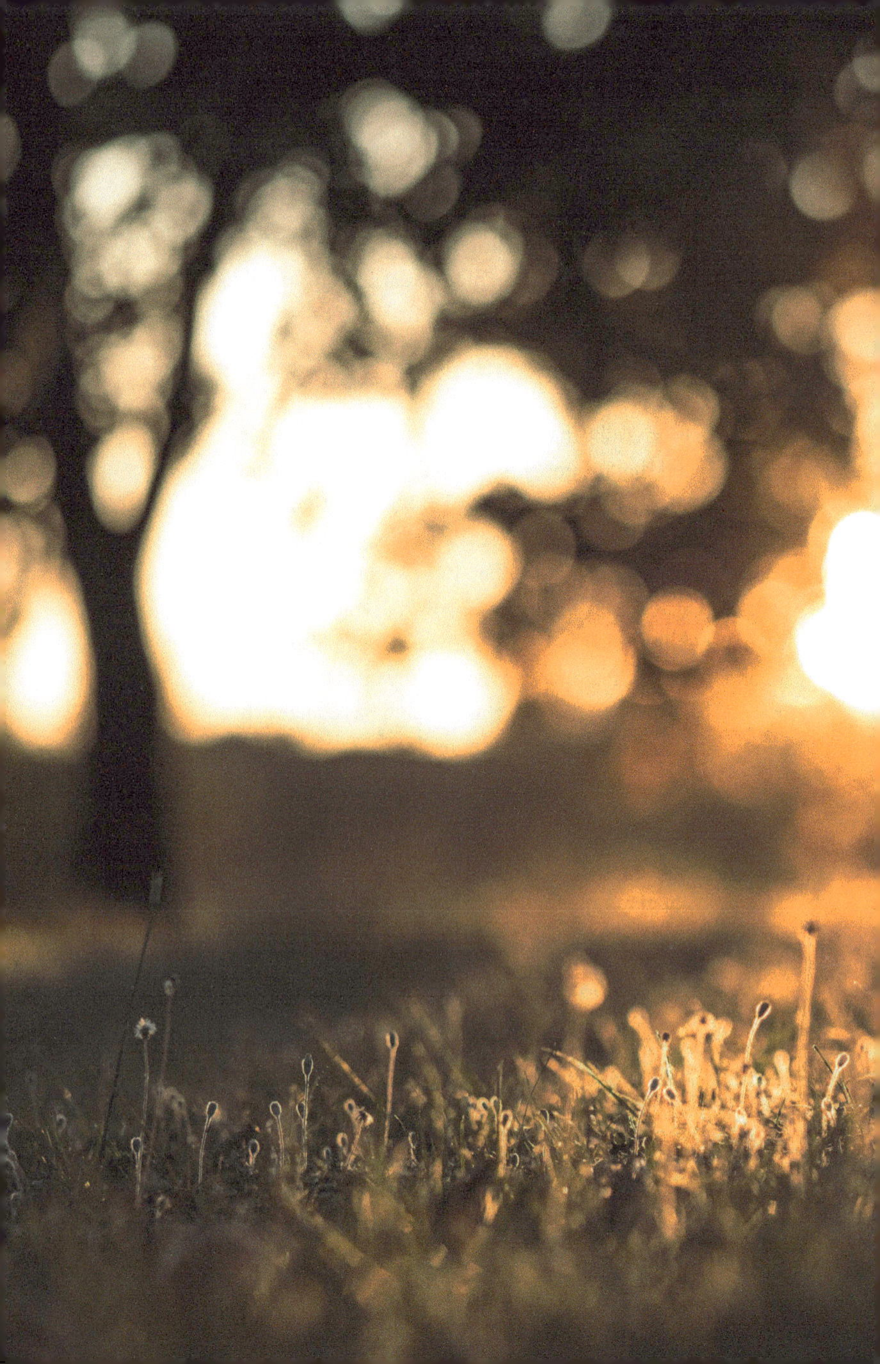

for social and transcendent realities: the call is bigger than I am, although it includes me. Within the logic of gift, we do not create our lives; instead, we are called and summoned by life.[15]

Keeping in touch with God's call (or for the non-believer, one's sense of self or purpose) requires time for reflection, listening, and wonder.

A Sabbath recentres us in many ways. In part, its importance for the religiously observant is devotional: it is a day when we remember we are all equal before the Lord. But it also demonstrates for all of us that we are not defined by what we do or what we consume. We are free to be, rather than to do; and defined by being, not doing. Ideally, it can relieve our anxieties and create a sense of security, respect and dignity.[16]

Sustainability

Acknowledgement of the meaning of Sabbath as rest might also lead us to a greater appreciation of our need to rest the planet if we are to protect it. The verses from Exodus above states that everything is to rest and have time to recover on the Sabbath, including our livestock. Moreover, Leviticus 25:1–7 reminds us that there is a clear principle to rest the land as well every seven years. Through patterns of rest, we rediscover humanity's common place as part of (not separate from) the natural world.

> **The additional constraint of the planet must form part of our consideration of how we limit and shape future work.**

Given the importance of the ecological wave discussed at the outset, the additional constraint of the planet must form part of our consideration of how we limit and shape future work. For too long, the provision of jobs in the pursuit of growth in all sectors of the economy, including agriculture, has neglected the care of the earth. Concretely, this requires a better assessment of the specific contribution of each job or human activity by each worker to the care of our common home.

Rest versus leisure

All this raises the question of what we take time off *for* – and especially the distinction between rest and recovery, and leisure and enjoyment. Rest is what we do to allow the body, mind, and soul to repair and restore itself to prepare for activity and the expenditure of energy. Leisure looks more like refreshment: it nourishes as well as restores. Amusement, in contrast, tends to be used for forgetting rather than refreshing, and is often – think of smart devices and video games – a means of escape and a way to lose oneself instead of finding oneself.

For all these reasons, all humans need the "right to switch off". The point and the justification of leisure is to enable us, as human beings to: retain our humanity; flourish as people and in community; have the time and perspective to understand what matters most.

Of course, there exists a clear way to switch off, and that is the Sabbath, a habit of rest, leisure, and worship that has lost much of its currency in recent times.

By letting the practice of the Sabbath slip away from us, we have lost time for the reflection and recentring that it brings. If we do not find time to put aside regularly to enable us to keep on a nodding acquaintance with our internal drivers, rather than be defined by forces outside of us, we lose resilience and we suffer. For many, the decrease in "busyness" engendered by the pandemic has given them more time for reflection and consideration of what matters most to them. This has been an unintended, and strongly positive, consequence for many people. Hopefully, as life gears back up, we will be able to hold on to some of the better habits we have established over this period.

Towards more balanced lives

The problem is not simply how to live, but how to live well. We will be forced to consider what it really means to live a meaningful life. The need for leisure in our lives is clear, as is the need to make time for all the things that permit us to flourish: family, community, and hobbies. We each seek to achieve life's full potential: increase our positive emotions, engage with the world and our work (or hobbies), develop deep and meaningful relationships, find meaning and purpose in our lives, and achieve our goals through cultivating and applying our strengths and talents.

Yet most of us still need to earn the means by which to live, and all of us have obligations or chores that need to be done to maintain our daily lives. And the day has only 24 hours. How do we rediscover the balance and wholeness that comes from a consistently kept period of worship and leisure in the modern world? Those on the margins, who must work two or even three part-time jobs in order to feed their families, get no time at all to rest.

If Sabbath is rest – the Hebrew word literally means "stop" – then it points towards the restorative trusting in God's provision that is receiving life as a gift. This does not suggest we need do nothing. Rather, it means that we need to examine the weight we are giving to production and consumption in our lives. It also means we need to consider which work is of most value. Housework, caring for others, and volunteering to serve or educate others can be every bit as difficult and time-consuming as paid work. However, we need to think of them differently as far as their contribution to a life of meaning and purpose, and contribution to bringing about God's kingdom on earth.

Below are some possible actions that could each, in their way, bring people closer to a more balanced life, particularly when combined with changes to pay, conditions, and a more humanised workplace.

First, we need to change the culture of work in most work places. This cultural element emerged strongly from our roundtable discussions. Jobs need to be defined to be able to be done well in the time that is allotted to them. The algorithm that tells the checkout worker he is not scanning groceries fast enough should not be driving what acceptable performance looks like any more than the Goldman Sachs recruit should feel she has to put in 95 hours a week to make the grade. The ability to limit work is not just an issue of the individual but it is a result of the entire workplace culture that needs to be reconsidered. Not only would this benefit the worker, it would likely result in lower absenteeism and illness (including mental health issues).

One measure that likely would force such a change in culture would be measures to enforce the payment of overtime. This would force employers and managers to carefully consider the boundaries between work and non-work time, and give them an incentive to observe them more closely. Another is the practice by Daimler of deleting employee emails that arrive during their holidays so that they do not feel obliged to check email on holiday. Similar moves should be considered so that emails only arrive during work hours.

Second, the increased use of flexible working would permit most people to incorporate more non-work activities in their days without necessarily losing work productivity. Shorter days and flexible working would also permit the older workforce to work longer if they so choose, going some ways to alleviating both the pension provision issue and the longer-term demographic challenges in the UK. It can also help them give back some of their time to their communities in volunteering, improving both social interaction and often health and mental well-being, as they shift from formal careers or jobs. The pandemic has demonstrated that many people benefit from working flexibly, so much so that many companies are considering adopting flexible working as people begin to return to the office. Employees in the UK already have a limited right to request flexible work. It may be necessary to review existing legislation based on progress on this front in the next year.

The benefits of volunteering for both the volunteer and the organisation they help cannot be understated. The balance of benefits differs across individuals. For example, younger people are most likely to highlight the importance of acquiring new skills and enhancing employment prospects, while older volunteers see the benefits from increased social interaction and improved health. But enjoyment and satisfaction rank high across all volunteer types.

One way to do this would make volunteerism an essential part of workers' contracts. Many companies currently allow a day or so a year towards community projects. This kind of tokenism needs to be changed to regular, consistent opportunities to do something beyond their workplace. This would permit community organisations to count on such help, and would work towards both providing the better-rounded day, less dependence on employment for satisfaction, and possibly even some skills building. A second way would be to add volunteering hours to state social insurance worked hours credits. This way, volunteers would benefit by building their statutory retirement provision.

An additional benefit would be that a renewed focus on volunteering would lead to greater consideration of the importance of "third spaces" that are neither work nor home: churches, sports, and social clubs amongst others. These have been squeezed by rising demands of workplace, particularly for those with long commutes. Not only do they build community, they add balance to life.

Third, we should consider how we can embed social practices of rest and recuperation. Presumably, there will be no return to strict Sunday observance and shop closures. We need, however, to consider how we offer secular "cultural jigs" which push people towards rest. The UK, for instance, has the fewest number of public holidays of comparable economies, and political parties have promoted the idea of using national saints' days as bank holidays. Measures can be easily taken to shift us towards an average in comparable economies.

> **The UK has the fewest number of public holidays of comparable economies.**

We need to use our leisure to think hard about what really matters. Consider the possibility of a "technology fast" one day a week. Think about those activities that enable us to nourish and shelter ourselves and our families and those activities that enable us to nourish our spiritual needs. Some people may find spiritual nourishment in their work, in this case very much their "calling". Others will find their spiritual nourishment in family, community, or a pastime, or a mix of those things, and choose to separate spheres between what they do to provide a living and what makes them thrive. The objective is that each human has the freedom to find that balance. This involves education, equality of opportunity, and the payment of a living wage for all jobs (and for people unable to work). It would be a mistake either to overvalue or undervalue our work and its place in our lives. A combination of changes to our working culture, changes to the wages and the hours of work needed to provide the necessities of life, and time to understand and enjoy the gifts we have been given may, with practice, permit us to achieve the genuine integration that leads to human flourishing.

1 John Maynard Keynes, *Essays in Persuasion* (New York: W. W. Norton & Co., 1963), pp. 358–373.

2 "Average weekly hours fell faster between 1946 and 1979 than post-1980", New Economics Foundation, 7 March 2019, www.neweconomics.org/2019/03/average-weekly-hours-fell-faster-between-1946-and-1979-than-post-1980

3 Robert Skidelsky, "How to achieve shorter working hours", (London: Progressive Economy Forum, 2019), www.progressiveeconomyforum.com/wp-content/uploads/2019/08/PEF_Skidelsky_How_to_achieve_shorter_working_hours.pdf

4 Calculated from average of quarterly data from the Office of National Statistics' Labour Market Overview, 21 May 2021. LMS measures all overtime and doesn't distinguish between paid and unpaid, www.ons.gov.uk/employmentandlabourmarket/peopleinwork/employmentandemployeetypes/bulletins/uklabourmarket/may2021

5 "Workers in the UK put in more than £35 billion worth of unpaid overtime last year – TUC analysis", TUC, 1 March 2019, www.tuc.org.uk/news/workers-uk-put-more-ps32-billion-worth-unpaid-overtime-last-year-tuc-analysis

6 The changes being made by British Gas include extending engineers' working hours from 37 to 40 per week; asking engineers to begin their working day in the customer's home rather than their own home; and the removal of higher rates of pay for weekend and bank holiday work. See Ashleigh Webber, "Crunch time for British Gas engineers to agree new contract terms", *Personnel Today*, 14 April 2021, www.personneltoday.com/hr/british-gas-fire-and-rehire-gmb-union/

7 "Workforce burnout and resilience in the NHS and social care", House of Commons Health and Social Care Committee, Second Report of Session 2021–22, 18 May 2021, p. 5, www.committees.parliament.uk/publications/6158/documents/68766/default/

8 Adam Smith, "Amazon will monitor delivery drivers with AI cameras that know when they yawn", *The Independent*, 4 February 2021, www.independent.co.uk/life-style/gadgets-and-tech/amazon-ai-cameras-yawn-drivers-b1797528.html

9 Private conversation with PWC partner.

10 Madeleine Bunting, *Willing Slaves: How the Overwork Culture is Ruling Our Lives* (London: Harper Perennial, 2001), p. xxiv.

11 Michael J. Naughton, *Getting Work Right* (Stuebenville: Emmaus Road, 2019), pp. 29–30.

12 Matthew Crawford, *The World Beyond Your Head: How to Flourish in an Age of Distraction* (London: Viking, 2015).

13 Walter Brueggemann, *Sabbath as Resistance: Saying no to the culture of now* (Louisville, Kentucky: Westminster John Knox Press, 2017), preface.

14 Naughton, *Getting Work Right*, p. 39.

15 Naughton, *Getting Work Right*, p. 40.

16 Brueggemann, *Sabbath as Resistance*, p. 27.

17 "Care is work; Work is care", Report of the Commission, The Future of Work: Labour After Laudato Si, p. 18, www.futureofwork-labourafterlaudatosi.net/2020/12/09/care-is-work-work-is-care-9-december-2020-global/

18 David Susskind, *A World Without Work*, (London, Allen Lane, 2020) p. 237.

19 Brueggemann, *Sabbath as Resistance*, p. 101.

20 Dr Abigail Gilbert and Anna Thomas, "The Amazonian Era: How algorithmic systems erode good work", Institute for the Future of Work, May 2021, p. 12, www.uploads-ssl.webflow.com/5f57d40eb1c2ef22d8a8ca7e/60afae719661d0c857ed2068_IFOW%20The%20Amazonian%20Era.pdf

21 Courtney Connley, "This company has an ingenious way to free employees from email on vacation", CNBC, 17 August 2017, www.cnbc.com/2017/08/17/one-companys-genius-way-to-free-employees-from-email-on-vacation.html

22 Andy Haldane, "In giving, how much do we receive?", p. 9.

23 Brueggemann, *Sabbath as Resistance*, p. 33.

Conclusion

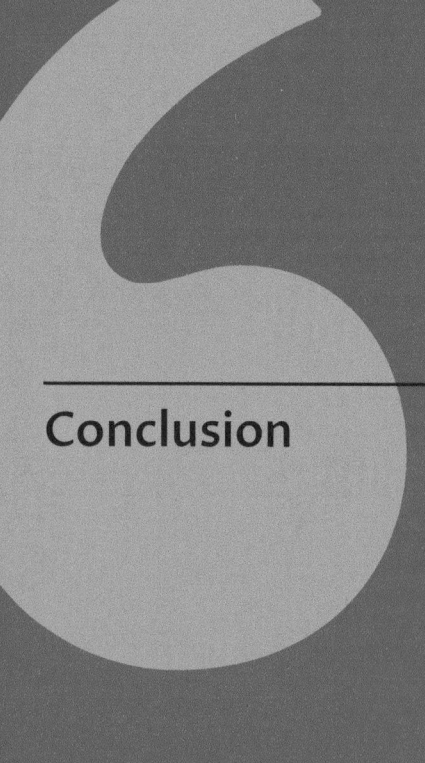

We started this report by outlining the technological, ecological, and anthropological waves which are disrupting the world of work. Although some might feel that these waves move us in the direction of a post-work future, we have argued that we will continue to need work.

Why? Because work is not only our best means of sharing in common prosperity, but we also need to contribute to that prosperity, share in the community which work creates, and derive a measure of meaning, purpose, and identity in the workplace.

That said, we must look to protect workers during this great disruption. There is an opportunity to use the energy of these disruptive forces to improve the position of workers – and we must do our best to shape work in a humane way. However, this window of opportunity may not last for long, so it is important to mobilise thinking around these issues quickly.

In Chapter 3, we turned to a particular problem that has – given the experience of 2020 – come into particular focus. The relationships between work, work*place*, and working *time* are shifting. Although some workers welcome the experience of greater flexibility, the truth is that boundaries between work and non-work have become so blurred that they often disappear. This is to the detriment of workers, and the attendant problems (surveillance and privacy, mental health) are likely to become defining workplace challenges of the 21st century.

The goodness of work

As we find a way through present disruptions, we need to set ourselves an overall goal. In the past, governments

have aimed for economies of full employment. We propose a
modification: that **we should aim to be a full work economy**.
To reiterate, work is not merely employment. It is our
contribution to, and part of, common prosperity – this can
include employment, but is significantly broader than it.

In practice, **a full work society may mean creating
incentives for people to *move out* of the labour market for
periods of time and for particular purposes that align with
some public good.** Most obviously, we already offer people
paid parental leave. This is treated as a grudging necessity,
and is often socially stigmatised. But the principle is already
established, and statutory support could be offered for the
purposes of training, education or skill development, or
secondments into civil society.

In *A World without Work*, David Susskind writes,

> *In a world where life expectancy is improving, where workers
> would benefit from taking time off to retrain, and where people
> face substantial and irregular demands on their non-working
> time (to bring up children, perhaps, or care for elderly relatives),
> it is striking that the state has decided to only really provide
> financial support for leisure once most of life is over.*[1]

What if the state were to provide financial support at
other times of life, but for other recognised social goals? This
may, in turn, encourage employers to ask how they can make
employment a more desirable option.

A human future for work

Work – or should we say employment – is changing. Old
challenges remain (such as ensuring a living wage) and new
ones emerge, particularly around the place of technology in the
workplace. It will continue to be necessary for governments

to set a floor on many of these issues, and be responsible for ensuring that employees don't find themselves beneath it. We have to understand how incentives can be realigned, and how the relative influence of different stakeholders can be balanced. Worker solidarity in the form of union action, which is such a key feature of Catholic Social Teaching, will continue to be important, but unions too will need to continue to respond to the emerging context.

But the key question is, will the future of work be human or robot? We have suggested that there is plenty of scope for automation, since automation will also in some cases reduce the need for human toil. If predictions of the scope of automation are anything like correct, there will be a need for substantial state action to help those displaced from work retrain. The present government has opted to load all responsibility for retraining onto individuals, but the state and employers should bear at least some of this load.

We should not neglect to mention chaplaincy as an important way in which workplaces can be humanised. Even enlightened employers have an interest in worker productivity. Chaplains, however, have the freedom to supportively engage with people as people. Given increased attention to religious diversity in many companies, attention is being given to workplace chaplaincy.

> **Chaplaincy is an important way in which workplaces can be humanised.**

Limiting work

We have identified the task of limiting work as an emerging challenge. Some have already begun to respond to this (for instance, with campaigns for the right to switch off).

The nature and causes of overwork are complex, as are the responses. They involve changes at the level of the individual, the employer, and the culture. Alongside these, governments again must set minimum rights below which we are not prepared for any workers to fall.

As individuals, we need to first consider the place of work in our lives, and how to de-emphasise its importance in order to make room for other ways of finding meaning, purpose, and fulfilment – whether those are in other meaningful "works", or in leisure. But individual decision or will aren't enough to override the force of cues from society, law, or workplace culture.

Legally, the most direct way to accomplish this would be to limit the time spent on work, both absolutely and psychologically, the former by limiting working hours and second by effectively requiring time that is "switched off". To be able to work less and switch off, it is critical that all who choose to work can cover the basic needs of themselves and their dependents with a combination of wages and benefits.

In terms of society, we have abandoned religious norms around days of rest. Might there be new "secular" patterns which will help workers – and employers – set narrower limits? More shared days off – bank holidays – would be one way.

How will employers, however, be incentivised to observe limits? One route would be to restore principles of paid overtime, or establish them in settings where it has not hitherto been paid. This will force employers to think about the amount of work required, and whether a particular task is resourced correctly.

Changing the culture is perhaps the most difficult. How we redefine success from what we do and what we possess to thinking in terms of whom we help, how we care for God's creation, and the time to enjoy it may be the biggest challenge.

Changing work

We have argued at length that work needs to be humanised in response to the coinciding waves of change facing the world of work – but it's clear that no one actor bears all responsibility for this humanising change when we address questions through the lens of the common good. Some issues relate to the basic conditions and rights of workers, and the most obvious mechanism to address them is through legislation (in spite of a commitment in 2019, there was no employment bill in the most recent Queen's Speech). These include:

- Retraining in response to the technological wave will be vital.
- The distribution of paid employment may require significant nudges from government, tackling the significant amount of unpaid overtime in the economy.
- This in turn will likely require, as we argued above, the countervailing pressure of organised labour, which is affirmed by Catholic Social Teaching.

This is complex enough, but getting market pressure to operate to the benefit of workers is a greater challenge still. Consumers are increasingly aware of environment and sustainability, and in future may factor in social and labour conditions. More likely, companies will realise that they need to look to the health and well-being of workers if they are to continue to operate. Investors, mindful of the "s" in the ESG (environmental, social, and governance) agenda, should add clear requirements on the fair handling of wages, benefits, agency work, outsourcing, and employee surveillance to the social criteria they consider when investing. This should start with church-based investors.

Why work?

In her essay, *Why Work?*, written during the privations of the Second World War, Dorothy Sayers bemoaned the consumerism that had gone before.[2] The productive power of the economy was directed at the war effort, and the nation had been thrust back to the frugal morals of their great-grandparents. When it was over, would it simply "go back to that civilization of greed and waste which we dignify by the name of a 'high standard of living'"? Or would people seek an alternative future, where work would perform some other function?

Battered by the waves of change set out in the introduction, we are faced with similar questions, and our answers will be discovered in the tension of this phenomena of work which is both inherent to our humanity, yet frustrated and restless. In an era when automation promises/threatens to eliminate much routine work, when our economic model based on endless and damaging growth in consumption, and faced with the reality of declining relative financial rewards, it is no wonder that a post- (or even anti-) work sentiment has developed. Why work? Good question.

There is an answer. When they work, humans are being human – relating to the goods of creation and of other people in a generative way. But on a personal and social level, work is often deformed. We need to pay attention to the way particular working structures dehumanise workers. Some of these questions – basic issues around pay and conditions – are as old as the hills. Others, such as worker surveillance, have a distinctly modern flavour. Still others, like complex relationship work-time, place, and work intensity, are questions that have been forced to the front by a 21st-century pandemic – we can address them by reimagining ancient practices of rest.

1 David Susskind, *A World without Work*, (London, Allen Lane, 2020), p. 229.

2 Dorothy Sayers, "Why Work?", www1.villanova.edu/content/dam/villanova/mission/faith/Why Work by Dorothy Sayers.pdf

Theos – enriching conversations

Theos exists to enrich the conversation about the role of faith in society.

Religion and faith have become key public issues in this century, nationally and globally. As our society grows more religiously diverse, we must grapple with religion as a significant force in public life. All too often, though, opinions in this area are reactionary or ill informed.

We exist to change this

We want to help people move beyond common misconceptions about faith and religion, behind the headlines and beneath the surface. Our rigorous approach gives us the ability to express informed views with confidence and clarity.

As the UK's leading religion and society think tank, we reach millions of people with our ideas. Through our reports, events and media commentary, we influence today's influencers and decision makers. According to *The Economist*, we're "an organisation that demands attention". We believe Christianity can contribute to the common good and that faith, given space in the public square, will help the UK to flourish.

Will you partner with us?

Theos receives no government, corporate or denominational funding. We rely on donations from individuals and organisations to continue our vital work. Please consider signing up as a Theos Friend or Associate or making a one off donation today.

Theos Friends and Students

— Stay up to date with our monthly newsletter

— Receive (free) printed copies of our reports

— Get free tickets to all our events

£75/ year
for Friends

£40/ year
for Students

Theos Associates

— Stay up to date with our monthly newsletter

— Receive (free) printed copies of our reports

— Get free tickets to all our events

— Get invites to private events with the Theos team and other Theos Associates

£375/ year

Sign up on our website:
www.theosthinktank.co.uk/about/support-us